ANGELA LEVIN

# DIANA'S BABIES

KATE, WILLIAM AND
THE REPAIR OF A
BROKEN FAMILY

*Updated edition*

ANGELA LEVIN

# DIANA'S BABIES

## KATE, WILLIAM AND THE REPAIR OF A BROKEN FAMILY

*Updated edition*

This edition first published
in 2015 by Angela Levin.

ISBN 978-1517103293

Designed by Martin Colyer.

To my family

# Contents

# Introduction:
## A very proper family

IN TERMS OF MAKING AN ENTRANCE, THE ORCHESTRATED STROLL of Prince William and Kate Middleton, Duke and Duchess of Cambridge, to St Mary Magdalene Church on the Sandringham estate in Norfolk, where their two-month old daughter Princess Charlotte was to be christened, could not be faulted. It was intimate, regal, dignified, moving, beautiful to look at and laced with humour provided by Charlotte's older brother Prince George, who was nearly two. It also spoke volumes. Kate, who seemed to have lost all her baby weight, was dressed with impeccable taste in stylish cream by a favourite designer, Alexander McQueen, and looked totally appropriate for a senior member of the royal family. Baby Charlotte lay quietly in comfort in her Rolls-Royce of prams, gazing open-eyed at the lush green leaves on the trees above her. Prince George, third in line to the throne, displayed his own fashion statement for toddlers, which also signalled the continuity of the monarchy, by paying homage to Prince William's late mother, Diana, Princess of Wales. She had chosen an almost identical outfit more than thirty years previously for William to wear when visiting his new baby brother Harry for the first time. It was a touching act of William's devotion to the memory of his late mother.

George, obviously on his best behaviour despite constantly turning this way and that to look curiously at the crowds lining their path, held tightly on to his father's reassuring hand. William didn't stop beaming. And no wonder. At one level they made a typical family unit, replicated throughout the world and marking an important milestone for any father. But for William it was an extraordinary achievement and a time of internal jubilation. His own family of 'one and a spare', as the British aristocracy describes two children, had secured the throne for another generation, but on a personal level the casual stroll symbolised much more. He had now also finally broken away from his dysfunctional past.

The birth of a first child means any adult will never be the same again. Whatever William had anticipated about fatherhood, the reality was inevitably going to be different and like other first-time parents he and Kate learnt as they went along. It's been that way since their relationship became serious. William taught Kate much about the demands of being royal, while she introduced him to the comfort and ease of a warm family life and middle-class values. Both have been on a unique learning curve.

Although no one knows what the future will bring, a basis of love and support is the best start. Kate understands William's needs and bends to his wishes. He wants to protect her so she never feels the isolation his mother did, and he has insisted on changes to the royal way things are done. Even the normally intransigent royal courtiers who contributed to making Diana's life so unhappy have had to bend to his wishes. As a result, William has the lifestyle he wants, while Kate has become more regal. Prince George's christening was an important milestone but the second time around meant they felt more relaxed and had no qualms about doing it their way.

Many of the choices William and Kate made for Charlotte's christening, in July 2015, showed a woman's touch; doubtless they spent hours discussing the finer details and coming up with ideas. It was a powerful example of how Kate understands William's needs and is happy to go along with them.

William had two priorities. The first was that it was an intimate family event as well as a royal occasion with the expected crowds and media frenzy. The other was that his mother, who would have been 54, was honoured and not forgotten. There were so many echoes of Diana at the ceremony that it was as if the baby's late grandmother had helped plan it. Diana herself was christened in the same church in 1961, and William wanted Charlotte's christening to be as close as possible to July 1, his mother's birthday. The baby princess was christened on July 5, just four days later.

It is often rumoured that William does not get on with some members of the royal family, and his insistence that the event was kept small and intimate meant that neither of his uncles, Prince Andrew and Prince Edward, were invited. Nor were his aunts, Princess Anne and the Duchess of Wessex, or any of his paternal cousins including Princesses Beatrice and Eugenie. William gets on well with Zara, Princess Anne's daughter, and she is a godmother to Prince George. The most welcome guests were Kate's parents, Carole and Michael Middleton, who had been staying with William and Kate at Amner Hall, the couple's secluded 100-room Georgian manor in Norfolk, about a mile down the road.

The private service, conducted by the Archbishop of Canterbury, Justin Welby, with the Reverend Canon Jonathan Riviere, the local rector, lasted just half an hour. Vaughan Williams's Prelude on Rhosymedre was played, as it had been at Charles and Diana's and William and Kate's weddings, as well as Diana's funeral. The baby was named Charlotte Elizabeth Diana. Royal babies are traditionally given four names, but William and Kate believed three were enough.

The Queen wanted to host the subsequent tea party in the baronial ballroom at Sandringham, no doubt to make the christening a more royal event. William agreed. Philip Rhodes, senior page at St James's Palace, who had the honour of carrying the official announcement of Prince George's birth, organised the event. The royal kitchens in London prepared light snacks, which were taken by road to Norfolk for the thirty guests. Three liveried footmen waited on the visitors.

WILLIAM IS KNOWN TO DISLIKE BEING CONSTANTLY IN THE public eye, but perhaps his pride in his young family is beginning to soften him. To everyone's surprise Kensington Palace confirmed that the public would be able to use their own cameras in the paddock outside the church. A Kensington Palace spokesman said: 'The Duke and Duchess have received good wishes from people across the country and they wanted to open the paddock to those who want to see their family. If people want to get pictures for themselves to enjoy then they are welcome to do so.' It was in total contrast to Prince George's christening at the Chapel Royal, in St James's Palace, when the public caught little more than a glimpse of the guests. Cameras were not, however, allowed within St Mary Magdalene church.

Two of Charlotte's godparents, Laura Fellowes and William's school friend Thomas van Straubenzee, have links with Princess Diana. Laura Fellowes, 34, is Diana's niece and William's cousin, and van Straubenzee's uncle Willie, known as 'Straubs', was a friend of Diana's family, the Spencers, from the 1970s. The other godparents are William's pal James Meade, Sophie Carter, a friend of Kate's, and her cousin Adam Middleton. The official photographs were taken by Mario Testino, the Peruvian-born photographer whose work Diana much admired. In addition Charlotte was borne to the church in an antique Silver Cross pram that was identical to one that both Princess Diana and Prince Charles were pushed around in as babies.

For Kate, who has always wanted children, the progression from single woman about town to mother of two has been nothing less than she anticipated. But for her husband, the odds for a contented family life were heavily stacked against him. As a child, William had everything that money could buy, but lacked what really matters: a secure, stable home life. The marriage of his parents, Prince Charles and Diana, Princess of Wales – she died tragically in August 1997 aged thirty-six – didn't stand a chance. Charles was thirty-two and under huge pressure to produce an heir, while Diana was naïve and just twenty years old when they wed. She was too needy. He was too reserved and emotionally disengaged. They had endless screaming rows, and both took lovers. It was a rotten blueprint to pass on to Princes William and Harry, but one that Charles and Diana inherited from their own parents.

Neither Diana nor Charles was given enough love, stability, and self-confidence in their formative years. Diana, who witnessed both verbal and physical violence between her parents, was badly affected by their eventual acrimonious divorce and grew into a hypersensitive and insecure woman.

Charles, meanwhile, had deep scars of his own, partly from the cold and distant upbringing from which most royal heirs suffered in the past, but also because Prince Philip thought Charles was something of a wretch, while the Queen put the needs of the nation above those of her family. Charles was required to maintain an almost permanent stiff upper lip even as a small boy, and there was little time or inclination for any form of intimacy between him and his parents.

Studies have shown that the behavioural patterns of dysfunctional families are easily passed down from one generation to the next. Family members believe that what they experience is the norm, and continue in the same fashion when they have their own children. Emotional mistreatment can have the same damaging effect as physical neglect, robbing children of a happy childhood and reducing their chances of growing into fully functioning adults.

William's dysfunctional family background gave him barely a clue of what a normal, loving family life was like or how it worked. His stormy childhood caused him to doubt whether he could ever be truly intimate with a woman or be able to trust her. Nor did either of his parents provide a model of fidelity.

William's situation is complicated by the fact that he is second in line to the throne, but his plight is common for an increasing number of children brought up in dysfunctional homes, whether in wealthy or poor families. Children instinctively imitate their parents' behaviour and how they interact as a couple, show affection, and deal with problems. William witnessed parents who could barely stay in the same room together.

No one doubts that Diana loved William, but as her marriage deteriorated, she leant too heavily on him emotionally. Even before her separation, she admitted William had become the man of the house, and called him her 'closest confidant' and 'soulmate'.

It is an unhealthy and damaging way to think about a child. A mother's duty is to care for her son, not the other way round; a son needs to be a child, and not his mother's best friend. Instead, Diana talked to William about her lovers and even took him through the complexities of her divorce terms before she agreed to them. Some people believe that Diana was a victim of the royal family. In reality, she was a victim of her own family and, in turn, made William a victim of her own behaviour.

William was only ten when his parents separated, far too young to take on a parent-like role and carry his vulnerable mother's emotional baggage. These terrible burdens were too much to place on a child who loved both his parents; he would inevitably worry that if he sided with one he would upset the other. Charles, on the other hand, was often absent, emotionally inhibited, highly self-critical, and laden with a sense of personal failure. When the marriage finally broke down in 1992 after eleven years, it caused a scandal. Diana had by then taken several lovers, and Charles had renewed his relationship with his old girlfriend, Camilla Parker Bowles.

William's experience of family life placed him, in theory at least, alongside society's deprived people. Dr Michael Niss, a consultant clinical psychologist in Johannesburg, South Africa, writes: 'Once trust of a primary relationship has been damaged, there is always the fear of allowing oneself to get too close to others – a fear of being hurt again.' William could easily have made an equally disastrous marriage, avoided commitment altogether, or, which would have been a disaster for the royal family, gone off the rails. Luckily, an instinctive caution stopped him from straying far.

He chose instead to marry his long-term girlfriend Kate Middleton, a willowy, 5 foot 10 inch, down-to-earth, confident young woman who comes from an ordinary, close, middle-class family. By doing so, William has decisively rejected what could have been his inevitable path, neatly side-stepped the more volatile and destructive tendencies of his damaged mother, and helped bring about his own redemption. No one should underestimate the willpower, self-knowledge, and courage he needed.

By 2010, he and Kate had been together for eight years, apart from a brief separation in 2007, and he had to face a major crossroads in his life. If he cared about Kate at all, he had to commit to her or let her go. He could propose in the hope of a fulfilled life and take the risk, however small, that it could all go wrong. Or he could let her go and continue to be wary and shield himself from being hurt. He had kept the lid on his feelings for so long that he would not have an easy time opening up. The alternative, however, looked very bleak. It was a battle between emotion and stiff upper lip, fulfilment and frustration, and his Spencer and Windsor sides. Luckily for him and for the nation, Diana's child let his feelings win.

Many children born into a similarly destructive family go under, but William has proved that by making the right choices, one can break the destructive pattern of family life repeating itself. The difficulty arises in working out what one needs to do and then determining how to do it.

Ironically, it was Diana who initially showed William an alternative lifestyle, something for which she deserves full credit. She was always determined to stretch his experience beyond that of most royal children and give him the opportunity and encouragement to observe how people outside royal and aristocratic circles behaved. William could have rejected this lesson, but has instead, since childhood, sought to be as 'ordinary' as his position has allowed.

But going to McDonald's or meeting homeless people could only ever provide a limited insight. What he really needed was an alternative family who could take him back to basics, become the model to help him understand how it all worked, and, as a consequence, enable him to salvage something from the wreckage of his parents' marriage. He found it with the Middletons, who welcomed him into their middle-class lifestyle. William loved becoming part of a warm family unit, and it was a novel and healing experience for him that Kate's parents got on well. It also gave him the chance to observe and learn how a settled, caring family works.

Many men marry someone who reminds them of their mother and perhaps William, 6 foot 3 inches, blonde and handsome, was tempted to find someone equally magnetic, alluring and captivating as Diana at her best. But he would risk that she might be a nightmare to live with. Crucially, in character and personality, stable, sensible, straightforward Kate is very different. Her other qualities include what she is not. She doesn't have aristocratic blood and didn't have a dysfunctional childhood, nor are her parents divorced. It might sound a little dull, but William has lived through enough turmoil to last several lifetimes.

By marrying Kate, William has drawn a firm line under everything that his parents' marriage represented, but he has not rejected either parent. Diana remains close to him, but in controllable, pragmatic ways. Kate wears Diana's engagement ring, and the young couple chose Kensington Palace, where Diana lived, as their London home. The birth of Prince George marked the start of the final phase in William's redemption. His behaviour has made it clear that he didn't want to pass on what he experienced to his children, and that he has seen and approved an alternative, more positive way.

Diana would have been fifty-two when George was born. It is difficult to imagine, as, like many who die young, she is freeze-framed in the public's mind as a young woman. While her ghost hovered over the arrival of both her grandchildren, Baby George's arrival also marked the start of a new era, not just for William and Kate but also for the monarchy. Perhaps sturdy George or Charlottte, whom William describes as 'joy of heaven', will inherit some of Diana's qualities and share ideals that Diana might have developed if she hadn't been so damaged by her parents. The crucial difference is that George and Charlotte will have a stable upbringing and a calm, loving home.

George's birth also signified that William, who is six months younger than Kate and was thirty when he became a father, had smashed the dysfunctional family paradigm that was his inheritance. His journey has been long and inspirational and is a remarkable feat for anyone, let alone for someone who is second in line to the throne and has little life that he can call his own. His obvious joy in family life, his relaxed involvement with both George and Charlotte and his support of Kate show that if he can manage it, so can others who have similarly destructive backgrounds.

How parents talk and behave in their children's presence is absolutely crucial in shaping their futures, establishing an emotional and moral underpinning that shapes their self-image and how they view the world and their place in it. Once this is created, it is very hard to change, so much so that when the children grow up and have children of their own, it automatically becomes the model they use. Being a parent is a difficult and demanding challenge, perhaps the biggest of our lives. It is far more difficult if the new parent wasn't properly parented and has no prototype to fall back on.

In order to understand the huge personal challenge William chose to tackle to discover what other children from secure, happy homes learn naturally and instinctively, it is important to go back to the past and highlight not just his own early experiences of family life, but also what his parents had been subjected to by their own parents.

When Diana was at her most troubled and volatile, Buckingham Palace feared that she could destroy the royal family. Now strong signs exist that William, in finding his own redemption, has saved it.

# One

## Diana's difficult start

❖

THE HONOURABLE DIANA FRANCES SPENCER WAS BORN IN THE
evening of Saturday, July 1, 1961 at Park House on the Queen's
estate in Sandringham. Her arrival was a huge disappointment
to her parents, but particularly to her father, Viscount Althorp,
who had been desperate for a son.

Johnnie Althorp, an equerry to King George VI and the
Queen, needed a male heir to prevent his land and title being
passed to another part of the family on his death. Diana's mother,
the Honourable Frances Roche, whom he married in June 1954,
had so far failed him miserably. She had already produced two
girls, Sarah and Jane, who were six and four respectively when
Diana was born. In January 1960, she did finally give birth to a
boy, John, but he was so badly deformed that he lived for only
ten hours. The death of a newborn is profoundly traumatic for
any mother, but Frances's grief was made worse when Johnnie, a
boorish and insensitive man, blamed her entirely for the tragedy.

Althorp's disappointment brought out a bullying streak
that first surfaced during his school days, and one that was a
characteristic of his father, Jack Spencer, the 7th Earl of Althorp.
Jack had treated his wife with cold indifference; Johnnie Spencer, who had seen little kindness at home, used this treatment
as his prototype of how to behave and was in turn brutal to his
own wife.

The marriage was never the same after baby John's death and when, eighteen months later, Frances gave birth to yet another girl, Johnnie made it clear she had yet again let him down. Baby Diana, however, seemed to know instinctively how to woo those around her. She captured her parents' love with her easy charm, a preview of her later ability to cast a spell over the world and particularly over men. Even her father took to calling her 'a superb physical specimen'.

Her parents' relationship, based on the traditional, formal pattern of the English upper class, improved briefly when, three years later, in May 1964, Frances at last gave birth to a healthy son, Charles, now Earl Spencer. The arrival of a male heir did not, however, heal the rift between the Althorps. Little Diana would sometimes tiptoe downstairs and watch, leaning over the banisters, as her parents fought verbally and sometimes physically, which had a corrosive effect.

By the time Charles was two, Frances, then still only thirty-one, was bored with Johnnie. She left him behind in Norfolk while she spent an increasing amount of time in swinging London. At one dinner party, she met and fell for forty-two-year-old Peter Shand Kydd, heir to a wallpaper fortune.

In 1967, after fourteen years of marriage, Frances told Johnnie she wanted a trial separation and moved to London. Diana, then six, and her siblings began the double life of children of separated parents, living in London with their mother during the week and returning to Park House at the weekend.

Children begin their lives by loving their parents unconditionally and find their separation deeply traumatic, as they are too young to understand the complexities of adult relationships. All they know is that their mummy and daddy are no longer together and, just as importantly, that one or the other is not with them. Children are, however, susceptible to atmosphere; they sense when a parent is stressed or sad and often blame themselves. They long for their parents to get back together and live happily ever after. When this doesn't occur, they feel responsible for keeping each parent happy, but inevitably don't have the experience to know how.

The fact that marital breakdown is now so common doesn't make it any easier for children. It shatters the core of their identity and the world they know, and they find it difficult to feel safe. If the divorce is acrimonious, their love for each parent will be challenged, and they can feel desperate for each parent to love them still.

Separated parents who put their children's needs first rather than their own will try to make the children feel secure and loved. Diana and her siblings were, however, merely pawns in their parents' war and the fallout left her with major psychological problems in later life.

Frances's action marked the beginning of an acrimonious period that must have exceeded her worst nightmares. Divorce was unthinkable in Johnnie's circles at the time, and when he got over the shock he became intent on revenge. Frances began legal proceedings for the custody of the children and the dissolution of the marriage. The case was heard on December 12, 1968. In those days custody almost always went with the mother but Johnnie, who, as was customary among upper-class men, had had very little to do with his children, fought the case with support from various well-heeled friends.

Frances's own mother, Lady Fermoy, who was furious with her daughter for blackening the family name, turned against her and testified that the children should stay with their father. The divorce was granted, with Johnnie awarded custody and Frances given access at weekends.

She then married Peter Shand Kydd, and three years later moved far away from her children to the remote Scottish island of Seil. This marriage too later broke down. The acrimonious separation made little Diana feel rejected, unwanted, and unworthy. Nor could she seek comfort from her two older sisters, who were by then at boarding school.

Johnnie, an unlikely single parent, had an equally old-fashioned view of child-rearing. Diana needed stability and reassurance, but was instead looked after by a succession of nannies and au pairs. One nanny banged Diana's head against the wall if she did anything wrong. By contrast, another, Mary Clarke, tried to get Johnnie to spend more time with Diana and little Charles. 'It was very hard going', she said. 'In those early days he wasn't very relaxed with them'.

He was often out at night, and the au pair or nanny put them to bed. Diana, at six, was left night after night with someone who was little more than a stranger while her father, who kept his distance at the best of times, was barely around and her mother was far away. It must, at times, have made her feel she was little more than an orphan. It is natural that a sensitive little girl like her would conclude that she wasn't important enough or good enough for either of them to want to be with her. Not surprisingly, her confidence and self-esteem plummeted. Try as she might in later life, she could never overcome her low self-esteem.

Diana longed for her mother, especially at bedtime to read her stories. She bravely tried to be a surrogate mother to Charles, but at night was so afraid of the dark that she was too scared to leave her bed and comfort him when he cried. 'I just couldn't bear it', she later remembered of her brother's sobs. 'I could never pluck up enough courage to get out of bed'. She saw it as a sign of failure, but trying to assume a parental role when she was so young damaged her further. She failed to remember the dangers of making a child into a parent when she leant so heavily on William.

As time passed Diana became increasingly rebellious and sulky, a warning sign that she needed attention. She took comfort in ordinary routine, something that William has also found therapeutic. She chose to wash and iron her own clothes, despite her older sisters leaving it all to the staff.

Diana's father sent her to boarding school at Riddlesworth Hall, near Diss, in Norfolk when she was nine. She didn't want to go, and felt rejected and anxious. From there she went on to West Heath, an all-girls private school near Sevenoaks, Kent, following in her mother's footsteps.

In the autumn of 1972, Diana's much-loved paternal grandmother, Cynthia Spencer, died. Shortly after, with appalling timing, her mother moved to Scotland. Johnnie found comfort in the totally encompassing arms of Raine McCorquodale Legge Lewisham Dartmouth, daughter of the romantic novelist Barbara Cartland, and a mother of four.

Raine's and Johnnie's paths had crossed at various social functions, but the two became much closer after his divorce. In 1975, on the death of Diana's eighty-three-year-old grandfather, the 7th Earl of Althorp, Johnnie became the 8th Earl, and his children moved with him to the historic Spencer family seat at Althorp House in Northamptonshire. Soon afterwards, Raine left Gerald, 9th Earl of Dartmouth, her husband of twenty-seven years, and moved into Althorp to be with the new Earl Spencer. Johnnie was besotted, but his children did not like her and were not invited to their wedding. Like her sisters, Diana cut down on her visits home to Althorp from boarding school. A stepmother is very difficult for girls in particular to handle at the best of times. Girls commonly feel that the stepmother has stolen their father's love and that they have been replaced by another woman in their father's affections. The marriage would have been another blow to Diana's self-esteem.

Johnnie's aunt, Lady Margaret Douglas-Home, said: 'The children looked so miserable. I don't think she (Raine) is made to be a stepmother. She must be the only pebble on the beach and wasn't willing to take second place to Johnnie's children'.

Diana's emotional life continued to be one of loss and rejection. After school and a brief time at a finishing school in Switzerland, she moved with three friends into a flat bought for her by her parents in the fashionable South Kensington district of London.

She became an assistant at the Young England kindergarten, in nearby Pimlico. In September 1978, Johnnie collapsed with a massive cerebral haemorrhage and was rushed to hospital. According to one doctor who looked after him, Diana was the most tearful of the three sisters and most strongly felt he would die. But against all the odds he pulled through.

The following year Diana caught the eye of the Prince of Wales.

## *Two*

# Charles's tough beginning

CHARLES PHILIP ARTHUR GEORGE WAS THE FIRST CHILD BORN TO Princess Elizabeth and Prince Philip. He was born at Buckingham Palace at 9:14 pm on November 14, 1948, weighing a healthy 7 pounds 6 ounces.

When Charles was three, Elizabeth's father, King George VI, died suddenly of a coronary thrombosis and the Princess, then twenty-five, became Queen. Charles, as next in line to the throne, became Duke of Cornwall. At the Coronation in Westminster Abbey on June 2, 1953, Charles, now four, sat quietly between his grandmother, now to be known as Queen Elizabeth the Queen Mother, and his aunt, Princess Margaret.

The dutiful young Queen devoted herself to her people in the United Kingdom and the Commonwealth, as she has done for more than sixty years. Her diligence, combined with the fact that she is not demonstrative and disapproves of those who are, has had a profound effect on her children, especially Charles.

Her iron self-control could easily be interpreted by a small child as coldness. If she had altered her work/life balance, and given more time to her family, Charles might well have become a very different man. But he was not high on the young Queen's list of priorities.

One of Prince Charles's former private secretaries told the author Graham Turner: 'If she (the Queen) had spent less time reading those idiotic [government] red boxes – to what effect, one asks? – and taken being a wife and mother more seriously, it would have been far better. Yes, she can handle prime ministers very well, but can she handle her eldest son – and which is the more important? If the Queen had taken half as much trouble about the rearing of her children as she has about the breeding of her horses, the Royal Family wouldn't be in such a mess now.'

The Queen had neither time nor inclination for childish chatter or problems. Charles was expected to be resilient both physically and emotionally, to get on with things and not complain. The author Penny Junor wrote in her biography *Charles: Victim or Villain?*: 'Never, not even as a baby, did he have his mother entirely to himself for any length of time'.

Decades later, the Queen reportedly said she felt guilty about her treatment of her son. A former senior courtier was present on one occasion when he overheard the Queen asking her husband: 'Where did we go wrong? And what can I do now? Charles is already in his forties'.

It didn't help that Prince Philip's own childhood had also been dysfunctional and unstable. His father, Prince Andrew of Greece and Denmark, was a philanderer, while his mother, Princess Alice of Battenberg, spent time in a psychiatric asylum and later became a nun. Young Philip was shunted round various relatives, who took it in turns to provide him with shelter and food, but little nurturing. However, he was proud to have virtually brought himself up and felt Charles should also stand on his own feet. Children who feel their parents have no time for them grow to feel that they are not worth their parents' love. Charles may well have felt essentially unlovable.

The Queen and the Duke of Edinburgh also chose to follow what was, even sixty years ago, an out-of-date approach to child-rearing. Charles lived in a two-room nursery far away from his parents. He was raised by stern nannies, governesses and tutors. His mother would see him for half an hour after breakfast and half an hour before dinner, but only when she was at home. He never ate meals with his parents. (Royal children were not permitted to eat dinner in the royal dining room with their parents until they were eighteen years old.) Not surprisingly, he grew up in awe of his mother rather than close to her.

When Queen Elizabeth took a six-month royal tour of the Commonwealth in 1953, she shook Charles's hand, instead of hugging him, when she returned. Reportedly, she would often visit her favourite horses in the stables after returning from a long trip before seeing her four children. Charles had a good relationship with his main nanny, Mabel Anderson, but it could never replace the unique bond between mother and child.

At nine, Charles was made Prince of Wales and then sent away to board at Cheam School, a preparatory boarding school in Berkshire. At fourteen, he was told he would follow his father's example and board at Gordonstoun, near Elgin in eastern Scotland. His grandmother, Queen Elizabeth, the Queen Mother, feared it would be a disaster and wrote to the Queen saying he would be terribly cut off and lonely in the far north'. She suggested he go to Eton instead. Philip, however, stood his ground. The school, which he had attended in the thirties, had provided his only security, and he failed to see that his sensitive son's needs were very different from his own.

Charles detested Gordonstoun, as his grandmother anticipated. He was relentlessly bullied and desperately lonely. He later described the experience as 'a prison sentence'. Being shunned, ridiculed, and terrorised throughout his teenage years left its mark.

He subsequently studied archaeology and anthropology, and later history, at Trinity College, Cambridge from 1967 to 1970. Soon after leaving university he met the uninhibited, fun-loving Camilla Shand, who was a year younger than himself, at a polo match near Windsor.

He was rather inexperienced with girls and was quickly smitten; she became his first, if not his only, love. He described her as a 'breath of fresh air'. They had a lot in common, including a love of the countryside, dogs, and horses.

Charles didn't grasp at his chance of happiness. Perhaps his most revealing admission came on BBC television in February 1981 following his engagement to Diana. When pressed by the interviewer on whether he was 'in love' with Diana, Charles replied, 'Whatever "in love" means'.

His relationship with Camilla lasted less than a year. Two years later, she married a well-connected cavalry officer, Andrew Parker Bowles. She remained friends with Charles, and she became someone he could talk to. Diana could not have been more different. The only thing the two women may have in common is that neither of them was the slightest bit academic. Diana left school without a single O level; Camilla managed just one. After Charles received his degree, he trained as a pilot with the Royal Air Force, then spent five years in the Royal Navy, where he qualified as a helicopter pilot, among other things.

By the time Charles reached his thirtieth year, the House of Windsor was increasingly concerned about finding him a suitable match and ensuring the next in line to the throne. He was selfish and craved being the centre of attention. Children who have never had enough attention or love when small display these characteristics. When they become adults, they don't feel they have enough of almost anything to share.

With perfect timing, Diana Spencer appeared on the royal radar. She was a bridesmaid at her sister Jane's wedding to Robert Fellowes, then the Queen's assistant private secretary, and the Queen Mother made a mental note of the shy, attractive, sexually inexperienced (royal brides were expected to be virgins) young woman.

Fresh, untainted blood from a family that was highly rated in aristocratic circles with a title that dated back to 1603 could solve the problem of what to do about Charles.

The Queen Mother discussed the possibility of a match with a friend and Lady of the Bedchamber, Lady Fermoy, Diana's maternal grandmother. Ruth Fermoy was thrilled. The proposed match would be the perfect way to repair the significant dent in the family's reputation caused by her daughter's divorce. Little, if any, notice was taken of Diana's troubled background.

At the time, Diana was a nursery school assistant, a good choice of job for someone so damaged by her troubled past. Little children can be healing, and those in Diana's care responded to her natural kindness. Perhaps they even sensed a kindred spirit. Fate decreed she would move on far too fast, before working at the school could begin to help her. When she wasn't working she enjoyed escaping from reality by reading romantic fiction, and rarely thought through the consequences of her actions. The Queen Mother then spoke to Charles, and royal invitations to Diana followed in quick succession, including one to Charles's thirtieth birthday celebrations and one to spend a weekend at Balmoral Castle, the Queen's private residence in Scotland. Romance blossomed. Diana, now nineteen, fell head over heels in love with her prince, who romantically sent her bouquets of flowers and spent hours talking on the phone. If she had thought about questioning what her future life would be like, she may well not have known who or exactly what to ask.

Within weeks, Charles was asking his friends whether he should marry her. Many thought he should not, as they had nothing in common and the age difference was too great. Camilla was still in Charles's life and had even found Highgrove House, in Gloucestershire, as the perfect country retreat for him.

If there were niggling doubts right from the start about Diana's suitability, Charles, under pressure, chose to ignore them. He proposed in February 1981, and Diana accepted. Significantly, Diana developed the eating disorder bulimia, which involves binge-eating and self-induced vomiting, shortly afterwards. The illness, which she kept secret for years, is complex and can be a response to pressure and a sign of low self-esteem, and it can be a cry for attention when emotional needs are not met. The disorder also becomes a way of expressing what the sufferer doesn't dare articulate, which is usually: 'I need to be taken care of'. Equally significantly, bulimics feel they will never be happy.

Diana described her suffering movingly in the BBC 'Panorama' interview in November 1995.

> You inflict it (bulimia) upon yourself because your self-esteem is at a low ebb and you don't think you're worthy or valuable. You fill your stomach up four or five times a day – some do it more – and it gives you a feeling of comfort. It's like having a pair of arms around you, but it's temporary. Then you're disgusted at the bloatedness of your stomach, and then you bring it all up again.

It is a tragic insight into her loneliness and exposes her desperation to be loved.

She also revealed that the illness took hold soon after her engagement, a time which should have been the happiest of her life: 'I think like any marriage, especially when you've had divorced parents like myself, you'd want to try even harder to make it work and you don't want to fall back into a pattern that you've seen happen in your own family'.

Children of warring parents have little or no idea how to make a marriage work. They can try too hard, while at the same time being too demanding and continually making their partner's actions be a judgment of their own worth. It makes them difficult to live with and sets up a vicious circle of recrimination and ultimatums.

Nor did the intense media attention help. Diana added, 'It started to focus very much on me, and I seemed to be on the front of a newspaper every single day, which is an isolating experience, and the higher the media put you, place you, the bigger the drop'.

The dynastic wedding, a day of celebration and relief, took place on July 29, 1981 at St Paul's Cathedral. Diana wore a puffball meringue wedding dress and a tiara that was a Spencer family heirloom and, she said, gave her a headache. Charles wore his Navy commander's uniform. The press labelled it a 'fairy tale wedding' and the 'wedding of the century', and an estimated global TV audience of 750 million watched the wedding. In retrospect, it all seems a bit of a fraud. The realistic chances of a successful union were minute. Charles was old for his years, idiosyncratic and deeply introspective, with a tendency towards self-pity. Diana was naïve and damaged, with no idea that Charles's sense of duty, as heir to the throne, would rule his life. She yearned for something to fill the emotional void left by her dysfunctional childhood, while Charles had, since his childhood, kept true intimacy at bay.

The newlyweds' honeymoon was a two-week cruise on the Mediterranean aboard the royal yacht *Britannia*, ending in the Red Sea in Egypt. Diana began screaming at her new husband within days and spent much of the time in tears. Charles, very unused to such uncontrolled behaviour, didn't know how to cope with a woman who wore her heart on both sleeves.

Once home, Diana felt increasingly intimidated and uncomfortable with most of Charles's friends, particularly his horsey, polo-playing set. She tried to ban them and threw tantrums or sulked when she didn't get her way. She had a natural instinct for detecting freeloaders and sycophants, as many of those who hung around Charles were, but lacked subtlety in expressing her point. She preferred city life, shopping for designer clothes and eating in smart restaurants.

Her insecurities made her jealous of all Charles's previous female friends, particularly Camilla, whom Diana later famously obliquely referred to as 'the third person in our marriage'. She even became paranoid about Charles's correspondence with his mother, believing they were writing about her. Charles felt distraught that he couldn't make Diana happy, but remained loyal and didn't discuss her moods with anyone.

But as Diana's relationship with Charles declined, so her love affair with the public took off. The press couldn't get enough of her and in December 1981, the Queen summoned Fleet Street editors to Buckingham Palace, where her press secretary announced that 'the Princess feels totally beleaguered'.

It was a waste of time. Diana had an amazing ability to enchant and enthrall people of all ages and types and a limitless capacity to communicate and empathise with the vulnerable, sick, and dying. Charles was quickly aware of his wife's charisma and that the crowds wanted to see her and not him.

Rather than being thrilled and proud, he felt crushed and humiliated, and on more than one occasion was heard to comment, 'I might as well stay in the car'. Charles was used to being the centre of attention and found playing second fiddle to his glamorous wife deeply disconcerting. It must have evoked moments from his neglected childhood and made him feel unworthy. Her stratospheric progress to superstar and saint was not easy to handle.

Diana hated to be on her own and her behaviour at home was in stark contrast to her public appearances. She felt trapped in Buckingham Palace and would wander along its empty corridors, listening to her Walkman, and shutting herself away. She told friends she felt bewildered and lost.

The building was unfriendly and, astonishing and thoughtless as it seems in retrospect, the courtiers left her to her own devices. Instead, Diana was expected to know how to be a princess almost overnight. No one taught her how to cope, and she had too little self-esteem or confidence to ask for help. Not surprisingly, she felt she had been 'thrown to the wolves'.

Although she was completely out of her depth, she tried her best. She discovered a magic touch with the sick and dying, but had no idea how to cope with the aftermath of so much tragedy. She explained how she felt in the 'Panorama' interview:

'I'd come home feeling pretty empty, because my engagements at that time would be to do with people dying, people very sick, people's marriage problems, and I'd come home and it would be very difficult to know how to comfort myself having been comforting lots of other people, so it would be a regular pattern to jump into the fridge.'

William has ensured that this treatment would not happen to Kate. After their honeymoon, Kate was given private training at St James's Palace in London in many aspects of being a senior member of the royal family. This training included learning about the monarchy's long history; how the government and national institutions work; and how the media operates. It also covered the myriad small details of royal life, including when she should curtsy and when not to take a handbag. She was also introduced slowly and gradually into her role. Being mature, secure, and university educated, she happily asked lots of questions. Diana, who grew up with parents who put her low on their priority list, kept her anxieties, as well as her questions, to herself.

Diana's pregnancy was announced in November 1981, and both parents-to-be were genuinely overjoyed. Diana was very sick, partly due to her bulimia. She became hysterical over trivial matters and behaved increasingly recklessly. When she was three months pregnant, she threw herself down the stairs at Sandringham. She also self-harmed, cutting her legs with a penknife, and threw herself at a glass cabinet. Much later, in her famous BBC TV 'Panorama' interview with Martin Bashir in 1995, she admitted: 'I didn't like myself. I was ashamed because I couldn't cope with the pressures.'

Kate was also very unwell during the early part of both her pregnancies with hyperemesis gravidarum, a debilitating and serious form of unrelenting morning sickness. When she was pregnant with George, she was so ill that she was briefly hospitalised. It meant announcing her pregnancy very early and cancelling all her public engagements. Yet she handled it courageously and was back on royal duty as soon as she could.

About thirteen percent of women get depressed during pregnancy. Diana's marital problems, stressful life, and youth combined to make her much more vulnerable. The healthiest of women are prone to overreact, have a shorter fuse, and be excessively emotional once the pregnancy hormones course through their systems. The approaching responsibilities of motherhood can seem very daunting. Diana found it hard to control her emotions at the best of times, so it was particularly difficult for her. In addition, her mother had left her with a very negative experience of how a mother behaves. The responsibility of not just bringing up a baby but a child who would be a very senior member of the royal family was terrifying when she couldn't even cope with herself. It is not surprising she couldn't manage the pregnancy.

The prospect of fatherhood can seem equally unnerving for a man who finds it hard to share on an emotional or practical level, or for someone like Charles, who had been expected to bring himself up.

Prince William Arthur Philip Louis was born at St Mary's Hospital, London, on June 21, 1982, less than a year after the wedding. Diana's labour had lasted sixteen hours and Charles was by her side throughout. It was a royal precedent, but Diana had wanted him there. It was her way of saying she was determined to transform royal parenthood.

At William's christening ceremony, a sudden gust of wind caused the candle held by Prince Charles to flicker, but failed to extinguish it. Sir Laurens van der Post, the writer and mystic, who was one of William's godfathers, declared it was the sign of a crisis in his future, but one, he said, 'that he will survive'.

## *Three*
# William: A baby born in turmoil

NEWS OF THE SAFE ARRIVAL OF A HEALTHY ROYAL BOY REVER-
BERATED round the world. Hard-core royalists and the House
of Windsor were relieved and delighted that Diana had done
her duty by producing a baby of the right sex with impressive
promptness. A forty-one gun salute in Hyde Park and a ca-
cophony of bells at Westminster Abbey greeted the momentous
event. Charles gave Diana a diamond and pearl necklace and a
custom-built apple green Mini convertible.

Astrologers have, since William's birth, delighted in plotting
his character and predicting his future. Sally Brompton, a lead-
ing astrologer, noted that he was born under the sun sign of
Cancer just a few hours after a solar eclipse. He was, she said,
unlikely to suffer fools gladly and would have a tendency to grow
irritated and impatient when faced with situations he couldn't
control. He was thoughtful, sensitive, and compassionate, but
would worry about being trapped or tied down. His need for
emotional security would be paramount, as it was for his mother.

Diana felt euphoric when her child was born. Charles was
quite overwhelmed and wrote to his cousin Patricia Mountbat-
ten: 'The arrival of our small son has been an astonishing experience and one that has meant more to me than I could ever have
imagined. I am SO thankful'.

Any hope, however, that the couple would bond over the new

baby was short-lived. Diana's jubilation lasted only a couple of months, to be replaced by a disturbing postnatal depression. Charles agonised over what to do about his wife's hysterical weeping, mood swings, and increasing paranoia, and found a psychiatrist for her. She dropped his choice and found another, but then stopped seeing anyone after six months. She chose not to mention that she was suffering from bulimia.

Baby William was at last someone she could love unconditionally and might make the world right for her. It is a misplaced need to have a child because of what he or she can do for you; it is the child who needs looking after. The fact that Diana wasn't properly mothered when she was a child meant it was almost impossible for her to act like an adult once she herself became a mother -- she still needed someone to look after her.

Instead, she relied on her instinct and fortunately baby William blossomed. When he was nine months old, his parents took him with them on a tour of Australia and New Zealand. The Queen had always left her children at home when she went on tour, but Diana refused to go without William. It was a significant break with royal precedent and meant both first and second in line to the throne would be travelling together. The baby stayed with his nanny, Barbara Barnes, in Alice Springs, and Diana and Charles used every gap in their busy schedule to fly over to be with him, even if it was for just a few hours.

The reaction in Australia and New Zealand to the royal couple mirrored that in the UK. Diana was idolised by the crowds, whereas Charles's reception was only lukewarm. The tour was a triumph, enhanced by Prince William's first photo call in Auckland, New Zealand, where millions watched him crawling happily across a rug on television. The UK Government realised she was becoming a major asset to the country, while Buckingham Palace felt increasingly concerned about her unpredictability and mood swings.

The tour also showed that Diana was determined not to be an

absent mother. She was equally resolute that her son would have a broader experience of life and would do what ordinary people did. It sounds simple, but is in practice difficult to achieve for a world superstar royal.

She managed to take him to Selfridges, the central London department store, to meet Father Christmas. Instead of going straight to the front, or arranging a private meeting, she made him stand in a queue with the public. William, a toddler, wouldn't have grasped her broader intent, but perhaps it sowed the seeds that an ordinary life was worth seeking. It may have been his salvation; otherwise, he might never have given middle-class Kate Middleton a second glance when they met at St Andrews University.

William's first school was Mrs Mynor's Nursery School in multiracial Notting Hill, West London. Ken Wharfe, Diana's former bodyguard, remembered William's first day well: 'Even at that age, four or five, William was very concerned about his mother's relationship with the photographers'. His sensitivity to photographers in general and paparazzi in particular developed into a loathing, but he knows cooperating with them while he is on public duty is an inescapable demand of royal life.

How often the young boy overheard his parents' screaming rows as their relationship continued to deteriorate can only be guessed at. Their polar opposite personalities meant Charles continued to avoid talking about his feelings. Diana remained emotionally incontinent and very highly strung. Between official duties, Charles continued with his pastimes of polo, hunting, shooting, and fishing. Diana continued to shop.

Harry's birth in September 1984, twenty-seven months after the birth of William, did nothing to heal the widening rift between them, especially as Prince Charles let slip just after the birth that he had hoped for a girl. Diana was furious.

She enjoyed being a mother and spending time with her sons, playing, reading stories, and being around at bath time. As they grew, she made an effort to take them to nursery school, and she and Charles tried to turn up for school concerts and sports day. It's what normal parents do but was unprecedented behaviour for the royal family.

Charles even delayed an official engagement to see Wills, as they called William, play the drums at his school Christmas concert. Diana took both boys to see 'Snow White and the Seven Dwarfs' at a Leicester Square cinema and then treated them to a lunch of hamburgers and ribs at the Chicago Rib Shack, an American-style restaurant in Knightsbridge.

Many of their outings were splashed in the following day's newspapers. The world was obsessed with Diana, and anything the boys did attracted massive media attention. Although she had the best of intentions with regard to her sons, she just didn't have a stable enough background to enable her to fulfil these goals in practice. Gradually, the shadows of her corrosive past clouded her natural maternal instincts.

It would be naïve to imagine that William's time spent doing ordinary things represented anything more than a small slice of his life, albeit a valuable one. His destiny has inevitably set him apart and meant his life overall could not really be anything other than extraordinary.

He and Harry slept in a two-room nursery above their parents' bedroom in Kensington Palace, their London home; they had their own bathroom with a child-size basin and toilet. Their two nannies slept along the corridor.

From the barred nursery window, they could see the royal helicopter pad. William loved to watch the ground crew's arm signals. One of his first words was 'plane', a foretaste perhaps of his fascination with flying. Their toys were often gifts from world leaders and their wives. Nancy Reagan, for example, gave them a rocking horse.

Many weekends were spent at Highgrove, though Diana never liked it, claiming it was the home of another woman. Diana couldn't cope with the fact that Camilla had been a regular visitor. There little William could indulge himself with a £30,000 miniature Jaguar to drive, a present from the car's manufacturers. They also had several ponies.

William was known to throw temper tantrums, although whether this was an early character trait or merely copying his mother isn't clear. He was once ignominiously brought home early from a friend's birthday party after he reportedly screamed when he wasn't allowed to blow out the candles on the birthday boy's cake and then threw cakes and sandwiches round the room.

Diana affectionately called him 'Your Royal Naughtiness'. Harry, at the time, was quieter and shyer than his big brother. Fortunately for William and for the future of the crown, he is a good mix of Spencer and Windsor. He has inherited his mother's compassion as well as her looks, but also, crucially, his father's sense of duty. Charles occasionally involved himself with his children by taking them on nature walks and reading to them, things his own father had not done with him.

Cracks in the royal couple's relationship first appeared in the press in 1986 following a summer holiday in Majorca. Eagle-eyed journalists noticed that, when the couple spent the day at sea on Spanish King Juan Carlos's motor yacht, they didn't exchange a word. Instead, when Charles came up on deck Diana went below, and vice versa. The trip marked a growing coldness in their relationship.

When they were not performing a public duty, they lived separate lives and Diana's sense of isolation increased. Her relationship with her sisters, mother, and several friends was volatile. She saw conspiracies everywhere and took to leaving anonymous and rather unpleasant messages on people's telephone answering machines.

Perhaps this was the time at which William switched to becoming the only ally she could really trust and someone she could lean on, rather than just being a much-loved little boy. In doing so she placed an intolerable burden on him to be an adult before his time and as a result damaged his own childhood, when it was his need and right to be looked after. He did his best, but what is most awful of all is that, being a child, he could have no insight into what she was doing or how to help her, or even to see any flaws in a beautiful mother he loved so much. This burden put him under colossal pressure.

Children who feel a sense of hostility and lack of affection in their parents' relationship feel very insecure. It leaves them with a fear of intimacy and they shy away from a trusting relationship for fear that, if it breaks, they may have to face emotional hurt and trauma. Instead, they may chose a sexual relationship without any attachment, commitment, or emotional involvement.

Certainly Diana began to feel threatened by William's close relationship with his nanny, Barbara Barnes, and dismissed her. William was four, and was so fond of Barbara that he climbed into bed with her most mornings before breakfast. He so keenly felt her loss that more than two decades later he put her name on his personal wedding invitation list.

This touching gesture shows how much he needed and depended on his nanny to provide a stable element in his young life. Suddenly removing her from his existence must have hurt him to the core. He was also without his father for weeks at a time. Instead of trying to sort out his and Diana's marital difficulties, Charles escaped. In 1988, when William was six, Charles first took an African safari, then played polo in Palm Beach, followed by a skiing holiday in Switzerland and a fishing trip in Scotland.

Charles displayed the ostrich-like behaviour of someone trying to bury his feelings and avoid dealing with a crisis in the hope it might go away. When he was home, Diana found it increasingly difficult to keep her feelings under wraps. When Charles kissed her after losing a polo game, she immediately wiped her lips with the back of her hand.

The public, however, felt she could do nothing wrong. She was wonderfully photogenic and increasingly stylish. She had become a modern icon who exuded compassion and glamour in about equal measure and thrived on the adulation. Her photograph was featured on the cover of more magazines than that of anyone in history.

Her involvement in various charities, particularly those involving children, helped raise millions of pounds. In particular, she made a huge impact in 1985 when visiting a children's AIDS unit in Harlem Hospital during a trip to New York by spontaneously hugging a seven-year-old sufferer. The gesture helped change public attitudes towards AIDS.

Diana was brilliant at communicating with the disadvantaged. In one year alone, she visited seven shelters for the homeless. Everyone, it seemed, felt better for speaking to her. William went with her to the homeless charity Centrepoint in central London. It was part of her overall plan to show him how people who have nothing lived. The experience has stayed with him. 'I remember my mother taking myself and Harry to visit it when we were children', he later recalled. 'I was much younger, better-looking and naïve then, but it helped to open my eyes to the world so many young London people face'. In 2009, he slept under a cardboard box in the centre of London in sub-zero temperatures to gauge a little what it is like to be homeless.

Diana also went on four or five annual official trips overseas. But nothing could fill the void of her barren marriage. It might have stumbled on for many more years. But in June 1992, a book by Andrew Morton called *Diana: Her True Story* caused a publishing sensation. It was serialised in the *Sunday Times* under the headline 'Diana Driven To Five Suicide Bids by 'Uncaring" Charles'. It also referred to Charles's continuing relationship with Camilla Parker Bowles. Years later, it was revealed that Diana had given Morton six lengthy interviews while he was researching the book.

The book was published in the same month that William had his tenth birthday. It's hard to believe that the book didn't spoil his birthday, even if he didn't know that his mother had cooperated with the author. The next five years of his life were little short of toxic. The ages of ten to fifteen are crucial as children move through hormonally-heavy early adolescence towards adulthood. During this time, they need support and guidance as they gradually form their own opinions and values. Instead, William had to watch his parents tear each other apart.

The book's publication gave newspapers the green light to publish speculative comments about Diana's own relationships. They included James Gilbey, a sports PR; James Hewitt, an Army officer; Oliver Hoare, a married art dealer; and Will Carling, a married England rugby captain. Much later her friend Rosa Monckton revealed at Diana's inquest that she regretted her cooperation with the press.

Charles initially didn't believe that Diana had briefed Morton and felt they should stay together, regardless, for the sake of the country. It was not to be. On December 9, 1992, the then-Prime Minister, John Major, announced to the House of Commons that the Prince and Princess were to separate. The decision, he said, had been made jointly; they would establish separate households at Highgrove House and Kensington Palace. He added that they had no plans to divorce.

Many commentators saw the separation as Britain's most severe constitutional crisis since the abdication of Edward VIII in 1936. It irrevocably changed Diana's public image.

A couple of weeks later, the transcript of a private, intimate telephone conversation recorded in 1989 between the Prince and Camilla Parker Bowles found its way to the press. It was known as the 'Camillagate tapes' and gave details of Charles and Camilla's sexual relationship.

The separation was only the start of a battle for public sympathy that seemed totally to ignore the sensitivities of both their children. The boys were away at boarding school as their parents publicly let rip into each other on television with their own versions of their matrimonial story. It was more cringe-making than any soap opera. Charles agreed to be interviewed by broadcaster Jonathan Dimbleby for a television documentary, 'Prince Charles, The Private Man and Public Role', that was broadcast on ITV in June 1994, which 14 million people watched. In a subsequent book by Dimbleby, Charles admitted his infidelity with Camilla Parker Bowles, but said it happened only after the marriage 'was irretrievably broken'. William was twelve, an age when preadolescent boys can't bear to think that their parents have sex, let alone that their father has a mistress.

Although every child is an individual, they have certain common responses when parents sexually betray each other. The psychological issues can plague them for the rest of their life. Regardless of their age, children will feel many different kinds of emotions, including anger, anxiety, guilt, shame, and confusion. Many withdraw and become, like William, increasingly insular. They also feel pressured to take on the responsibility of winning back the love of the cheating parent or of becoming the surrogate parent of the betrayed one.

It was particularly difficult for William, whose parents' infidelity was played out in every media outlet.

Diana hit back hard a year later when she appeared on the BBC TV documentary programme 'Panorama'. Heavily made up with black eyeliner, she talked to Martin Bashir about her bulimia, self-harm, and infidelity. She admitted she 'adored' James Hewitt, who had taught her children how to ride, and that they had had a five-year relationship. Hewitt would later try to sell personal letters from Diana for £10 million.

This revelation must have been a huge embarrassment to William, and perhaps made him feel he had somehow been a party to his mother's deception by taking riding lessons with Hewitt. Diana also laid into Camilla with the words: 'There were three of us in this marriage, so it was a bit crowded'.

She seemed so self-obsessed and bent on hurting Charles that she hadn't thought to warn William, then thirteen and in his first year at Eton, what the programme would reveal. Instead it was Dr Andrew Gailey, William's housemaster, who read about the proposed interview in the press and persuaded Diana to make the trip to the school to tell William. She drove herself to see her son on Sunday, November 19, a day before the broadcast.

He was one of the last to emerge from chapel and walked with his head down. According to a photographer, William did not rush over the road to greet his mother. Instead, she crossed over to see him, then guided him behind a small hedge so that they could talk privately. The photographer related that William seemed close to tears and walked away, making no attempt to say goodbye. Diana drove off. The visit had lasted all of five minutes.

William watched the programme in his housemaster's study. It is difficult to imagine a more excruciating and painful scenario for him, or how a mother could be so insensitive about the way her revelations could affect her son. Twenty million people watched the programme, the biggest-ever viewing figures for a British documentary. The next morning, William was left in no doubt that the broadcast would be his teenage peers' main topic of conversation and the subject of crude jokes.

The Queen then decided enough was enough. After speaking to the Prime Minister, she wrote to both Charles and Diana to tell them to get on with a divorce. It was an edict, rather than a face-to-face caring conversation. She also encouraged William to make regular visits to see her at Windsor Castle, just across the bridge from Eton, and the Queen's favourite weekend home, for tea and hopefully some sympathy. A bond developed between them but it was one William risked breaking following his mother's death.

William also got on well with his grandfather, the Duke of

Edinburgh. They shared an interest in military history, and the Duke approved that William, unlike his father, enjoyed the outdoor life.

Their gesture was a silent comment on the inadequacies of each of William's parents.

# *Four*

# Divorce and a role reversal

If Diana had hoped to feel free of the controlling arms of the Palace once she was no longer living with Charles, it soon became obvious that the opposite was true. The press's appetite for gossip about her was insatiable, and it was almost impossible for her to go out on her own without being mobbed by reporters. She felt vulnerable and increasingly outmanoeuvred by the Palace.

She briefly escaped by going on a short, low-key tour of Argentina and then travelling to New York. The trip gave her breathing time, but didn't change anything. Meanwhile in London Prime Minister John Major, the Archbishop of Canterbury, and the Queen anguished over the constitutional nightmare of the failure of the royal marriage.

There was much to consider, including Diana's status and title, and where she would live. They also had to negotiate a financial settlement. Whatever they thought about Diana as a person, she was the mother of a future king. The Queen accepted that Diana genuinely loved the children, and decided she only needed to approve where William went to school and his choice of career.

The financial negotiations were a huge sticking point. The Queen is by nature thrifty, and she was shocked when Diana demanded a settlement of £17 million, not least because Charles's income from the Duchy of Cornwall in 1996 was £4.5 million and he wasn't allowed to sell any of the assets.

The warring parties were also at loggerheads over Diana's title. The Queen, supported by Prince Philip, was determined that Diana wouldn't keep the title Her Royal Highness (HRH), which shows the individual has a direct family connection to the crown and assures she will be automatically included in state occasions. Diana, however, was equally determined to keep it and be appropriately acknowledged as the future king's mother.

She won one demand and lost another. On July 13, the Palace agreed that she would receive her £17million settlement, plus £400,000 annually for her office. Her home with the children would continue to be Kensington Palace. She would no longer, however, be able to use the swimming pool in Buckingham Palace, and, more significantly, would henceforth be known as Diana, Princess of Wales, without the prefix HRH.

Diana was profoundly upset at the loss of her title, and much of the media thought it was a spiteful gesture. William, who had been kept up-to-date with changes in the negotiations, adopted a fatherly role as best he could, telling her: 'Don't worry Mummy. I will give it back to you one day when I am King'. It is a profoundly touching comment; it reveals how responsible the fifteen-year-old felt for her and that he had taken her worries on his very young shoulders.

Diana would no doubt have been horrified to know that turning her child into a surrogate parent was profoundly damaging, but the truth is that using William to protect her and respond to her needs was nothing less than exploitative. It is the type of behaviour that, when a child grows into an adult, leads him to believe that other people's needs are always more important than his own, that he always has to be mature or 'grown up' and, most significantly, that he cannot trust people to be there for him.

Nor was Charles jubilant that he was longer the butt of his wife's mood swings. He had tried his best to understand her but instead had made her desperately unhappy. He felt consumed with guilt that, not only had he been a hopeless husband, but he had also let down the Queen, the Queen Mother, Prince Philip, his children, and the British people. One of his few moments of solace was receiving a letter from his normally critical father, who wrote that he felt Charles had displayed the fortitude of a saint.

Charles had little time to wallow in his misery. His boys would be coming regularly to Highgrove, and he felt unable or unwilling to look after them on his own. So, shortly after the separation, he employed thirty-year-old Alexandra Legge-Bourke, affectionately known as Tiggy because she'd loved Beatrix Potter's stories as a child, as his personal assistant and part-time nanny. She was a lively, uncomplicated, adventurous upper-class young woman, who behaved more like a wild older sister than an employee. William, in particular, got on with her very well.

Diana felt jealous of Tiggy's appointment and believed that Charles was having an intimate relationship with her. Diana's judgement was so awry that she offended the Queen by initially accepting and then cancelling a personal invitation from her to join William and Harry at Sandringham for the traditional royal Christmas.

Christmas is a difficult time for children from broken marriages, and the Queen's offer was intended both as a peace-making gesture and a royal command. Diana couldn't face it, and, although her presence would have undoubtedly helped William and Harry enjoy the festivities more, she didn't put their needs first.

William's parents must have caused him such intense personal pain that he told both of them to stay away from Eton's Fourth of June holiday celebrations in 1997 and invited Tiggy to come for a traditional picnic instead. It was a sensible precaution to stop the event becoming a media scrum, and avoided the embarrassment of his being, yet again, the centre of attention and gossip.

Despite this, William enjoyed his time at Eton, especially as, unlike his father, he was allowed to choose his own friends. It helped that the royal detective who was always in attendance kept his presence unobtrusive.

Once Charles was no longer around, Diana made several changes at Kensington Palace. These included getting rid of cooks, housemaids, dressers, and secretaries, often on a whim. Instead she promoted her butler, Paul Burrell, to run her household and became increasingly reliant on him. Her clothes became sleeker and sexier, which would have been inappropriate for a senior royal. She also reduced the number of charities she was involved with from about 100 to six.

She had such a magic touch that many of the charities begged for her to do just one event a year so they could retain her name on their notepaper and keep donations rolling in. One of her greatest charity triumphs involved taking up the cause of banning anti-personnel land mines. Soon after her involvement, 122 governments agreed on a treaty banning their use.

Diana also found a new man to love, thirty-six-year-old Pakistani heart surgeon Dr Hasnat Khan, whom she soon called 'The One'. Wise mothers protect their children from meeting possibly transient men in their lives, but Diana introduced Dr Khan to William early on in the relationship and he stayed regularly at Kensington Palace. William liked him and spent an afternoon asking his advice on careers.

Diana began investigating mixed-faith marriages and asked William how he would feel if she married Khan, a Muslim. William reportedly replied that she should do whatever made her happy. It was such a loaded question that he had little option of saying anything else. She should have known better, and it was cruel and insensitive. It also highlights a huge gap in her understanding of the difference between confiding in a close friend who could tell her the truth and a young son who would be frightened of her overreacting if he didn't tell her what she wanted to hear. How could he be expected to know what that was?

The relationship didn't last. Dr Khan disliked the personal publicity and didn't want to offend his Muslim relatives. Instead of being protected by his mother from another failed relationship, William was left to face the loss of a potential role model. It was destabilising and another blow to his trust in adults at a critical time in his adolescence. He had also met Will Carling, another of Diana's lovers, which was particularly awkward as Carling was married.

William was then expected to cope somehow with his mother's feelings of rejection, isolation, and depression. His responsibility was all the greater as she was also estranged from friends and members of her own family, including the Duchess of York, who had herself just divorced Prince Andrew, the Queen's second son, and to whom she had previously been close. Diana's mother, who was drinking heavily, had offended her by publicly complaining about her going out with 'Muslim men'.

Diana also felt increasingly paranoid that individuals, including her brother-in-law Sir Robert Fellowes and Prince Philip, wanted her dead. She genuinely believed that the Palace was spying on her and that they would take away her children. She also found it hard to accept that, as England's future king, William needed to stay close to both the Queen and his father.

William bore the brunt of much of this turmoil. Diana told a TV interviewer that when he was ten, William played a parenting role as she wept behind a locked bathroom after a fight with Charles. Apparently William bent down outside, saying, 'I hate to see you sad', and stuffed paper tissues under the door. She related the anecdote, which must have caused William considerable anguish, with pride rather than with guilt.

In addition, she told Roberto Devorik, the fashion impresario, that she had 'very private and very profound conversations with him (William) and he was an extraordinary moral support'.

By now the mother/child relationship had been firmly turned on its head. It left William with a profound uncertainty about his role. He neither knew what was expected of him nor could provide the nurturing his mother needed.

It was around this time William began shouting at his mother a lot, partly no doubt because he was an adolescent but also because he didn't know how to cope. Nor did he like how mobbed they were by the press when they went out. When he was with his father on the royal estates, he had acres of freedom to do as he pleased away from the watchful eyes of the press. In London, with his mother, he felt cooped up, as there were inevitably many limitations on what she could do with William and Harry. He hated the media hounding and would have felt helpless and trapped under its relentless bombardment.

During the summer of 1997, much to Diana's dismay, Camilla Parker Bowles began to be slowly rehabilitated in the eyes of the public. Diana desperately needed a distraction; when the flamboyant and controversial businessman Mohamed Al Fayed, then owner of the Knightsbridge store Harrods and a friend of her stepmother Raine Spencer, invited her to bring William and Harry to stay at his villa in the south of France, she accepted immediately without thinking through the possible consequences. Charles, however, feared they might all be used by Al Fayed for his own purposes. His concern turned out to be more than justified.

Diana hadn't recovered from the breakup of her relationship with Khan when she flew out to the villa, but she cheered up when, three days later, Fayed's playboy son Dodi appeared, apparently at the request of his father. Diana was very vulnerable and easily captivated by his smooth ways. William and Harry felt uncomfortable with both men. When they left for Balmoral, she stayed on.

According to the author Christopher Anderson, Diana rang William every day while he was with his father and the royal family in Scotland to update him on the romance and see what he thought of her new love. It must have been extremely difficult for William to deal with while he was with his father.

For the next nine days, Diana and Dodi went on a cruise off the Sardinian coast on Fayed's yacht *Jonikal*. A wall of press photographers watched and waited, and the couple defiantly stayed on deck to kiss and rub sunscreen into each other. It was infinitely sad that she felt she had to prove her attraction in such an unsubtle way.

Some believe she was genuinely in love with Dodi, but it could equally have been a fling with the joint goal of drowning her sorrows over Khan and punishing the royal family. This time, her inappropriate behaviour ignited fierce criticism for subjecting her sons to yet another lover and, worst of all, to the influence of Al Fayed.

# *Five*

# Tragedy and loss

EVENTUALLY, THE COUPLE ENDED THEIR HOLIDAY AND ARRIVED IN Paris on the fateful afternoon of Saturday, August 30, 1997. The plan was to spend just one night there, as Diana wanted to get home for her boys before they went back to school.

Diana and Dodi were hassled by the paparazzi wherever they went. Shortly before midnight, they left the Ritz Hotel to go to Dodi's Paris apartment, just off the Champs-Elysées. Fayed's chauffeur, Henri Paul, who had been drinking, drove them. The paparazzi gave chase and Paul crashed at speed into a pillar in the Pont de l'Alma tunnel. He and Dodi died instantly. Diana was critically injured. A vital pulmonary vein, which carries aerated blood from the lungs to the upper right chamber of the heart, was torn and she died shortly afterwards. Neither she nor Dodi had worn a seat belt.

Diana had long had a premonition that she would die a violent death, but her fear could also have been due to her paranoia. Since her death, there have been countless conspiracy theories, and it took ten years before the jury at the British inquest returned a majority verdict that Diana and Dodi were unlawfully killed because of the gross negligence of their driver.

At 1 am on August 31, the British Ambassador in Paris rang Sir Robin Janvrin, the Queen's Deputy Private Secretary, with news of the crash. Diana had been injured but they did not yet know how badly. Janvrin immediately called Prince Charles and the Queen, who were at Balmoral along with William and Harry. The Princess died two hours later from severe chest and head injuries. Charles was devastated both for himself and for William, then fifteen, and twelve-year-old Harry, and didn't know whether to wake them immediately. The Queen recommended that they should be left to sleep and he listened to his mother.

Charles found it impossible to sleep. Instead he went for a solitary walk on the moors and anguished over how to break such devastating news to his children. He knew they would be heartbroken and their lives could never be the same again.

He rang his private secretary, Stephen Lamport, on his return. Even in his shocked state, Charles's sense of what would happen both immediately and up to the funeral proved to be correct.

'They're all going to blame me', he said. 'The world's going to go completely mad, isn't it? We're going to see a reaction that we've never seen before. And it could destroy everything. It could destroy the monarchy'. Lamport agreed.

Shortly after 7 am Charles went into William's bedroom. He was already awake and told his father he had had a very disturbed night. Charles gently told him that there had been a terrible car accident and that all efforts to save his mother had failed. William cried and wrapped his arms round his father. Charles hugged him in return.

William then told his father he wanted to go with him to Harry's room to help break the news. They woke Harry gently and, when he heard what had happened, he too burst into tears. Diana had been such a force for life and now she was gone. Charles told them that the Queen and Prince Philip wanted to see them; he took each of their hands, and the three of them went to the room where their grandparents were waiting. Neither hugged the boys.

Shortly afterwards, Charles told the Queen he wanted to go to Paris to collect Diana's body. The Queen told him not to, not least because Diana was no longer a member of the royal family. This time Charles didn't listen.

William then decided he wanted to go to church so that he could 'speak to mummy'. Attending Crathie Kirk, close to the estate, was an important part of the family's Sunday routine, and would be a comfort. Although the news of Princess Diana's death had instantly flashed round the world, the Reverend Robert Sloan made no mention of it at the service, much to the outrage of some churchgoers. He explained afterwards that he wanted to protect the young princes.

The royal plane collected Charles and Diana's sisters Sarah and Jane and flew to Paris. William wanted to go too, but his father refused to let him. Diana's body was laid out in a coffin. Her head had been badly injured and her face was distorted. Millions saw the plane land on television, but the Queen wouldn't let William and Harry watch. On Charles's insistence, Diana's body was taken to the Chapel Royal at St James's Palace rather than to the local mortuary in Fulham as originally suggested.

The national reaction to the news of Diana's death was overwhelming. The People's Princess had gone and the people mourned. Countless numbers made the pilgrimage to Kensington Palace to lay flowers, light candles, and leave messages of grief and loss. At the end of a week the field of flowers was as high as a small child is tall. The smell, a combination of fresh and decaying blooms, was intoxicating.

Individuals of all ages and types were initially too shocked to speak, and the whole area was wreathed in silence. Within two days, the shock had turned into grief and many openly wept. The grief was followed by palpable waves of anger, largely directed toward the Queen who, they believed, was staying 'on holiday' and keeping William and Harry with her when she should have come to London, shown her respect, and been with her people.

The masses, as Charles had foreseen, blamed him for Diana's problems and the failure of their marriage. A growing fear arose that the whole country was rising up against what was seen as the monarchy's coldness and indifference to her death. The Queen and Prince Philip, who had totally underestimated the strength of feeling, returned to London with William and Harry. They came back just in time, and public anger subsided.

Just before they returned, Prince Charles's press secretary, Sandy Henney, came to London to see the crowds on Charles's behalf. Henney recommended that William and Harry be gently prepared for what they would see at Kensington Palace. Charles accompanied them to the gates of Balmoral, where people had left more flowers and messages.

Harry grasped his father's hand and pulled him down to read a message. It was a touching show of intimacy and symbolic of how Charles opened himself up to his grieving children. The moment was pivotal. He would no longer always give in to protocol or to his own reserve when he was with them. It marked the beginning of a healthier and warmer relationship between Charles and his sons, and in turn loosened the thread of family dysfunction. Diana's death, however dreadful, might in some strange way have brought William closer to his father at a crucial time in his emotional development. Teenage boys need a male role model. Prince Charles had far too often selfishly focused on his own needs to the detriment of his relationship with William and Harry when they were small, but the tragedy of losing their mother impelled him to become more involved and to try to become a proper parent.

Perhaps too William felt a tiny measure of unspoken relief that, however great the tragedy, he no longer had to cope with his mother's hysterics or never knowing when her emotions would spill over and she would be reduced to tears of desperation. Nor would he have to deal with the terrible conflict of loyalty in his mind between Diana and his father.

Behind the scenes, more furious rows ensued over the funeral. The Spencer family and the Queen wanted a small private funeral. Charles insisted Diana have a full royal funeral at Westminster Abbey. The question also arose as to who would walk behind the cortège. Diana's brother Charles, now Earl Spencer, wanted to walk alone. Prince Charles wanted to be there as a mark of respect even though he feared that he might be lynched by the angry mob. William did too and defied the Queen, who told him not to. Harry wanted to join William, and Prince Philip volunteered to join them, not least as a physical presence between Charles and Earl Spencer.

On the day itself, the crowds that lined the streets to bid farewell to their princess behaved impeccably. All eyes were on William and Harry. No child should lose his mother and then have his grief observed by millions round the world. William, who had reached that awkward adolescent middle ground of being neither child nor man, had to think of the image he was presenting to the world rather than himself.

It would have been unthinkable to cry when the royals put so much value on a stiff upper lip. Nor could he grasp the reassuring hand of his father or grandfather. It wasn't the first time in his young life that he was required to behave like a man, but perhaps it was the first time he needed to act like a future king.

William moved forward slowly and with composure, from St James's Palace all the way to Westminster Abbey, his head bowed perhaps to avoid eye contact with anyone. Thousands lined the streets; many of them had slept overnight on the pavement to get their last view of their fairytale princess. The nation was awash with grief, which intensified when they saw the simple bouquet of white freesias on top of the coffin into which a white envelope had been tucked bearing the single word 'MUMMY'.

The deeply moving funeral service in the Abbey was conducted with the Palace's usual precision and style. Diana's unaccompanied coffin was a tragic, lonely sight as it was driven slowly through the streets to Althorp, the family home in Northampton, for the private burial service on a tiny island in the middle of a lake. Many who lined the streets threw flowers onto the vehicle. Charles, William, Harry, and the Spencers made the journey by Royal Train.

# 6
## William seeks his own path

THE LOSS OF A PARENT IS A DEVASTATING EMOTIONAL TRAUMA
FOR A child, and it was impossible for William to make any sort
of sense out of the sudden, totally unexpected death of his mother. One minute her warmth was there and the next it had gone.
William was used to her needing him. Now, instead, he felt a
painful emptiness. Life was never going to be the same again;
he had lost the most important woman in his life. He was aware
of her weaknesses and vulnerability but knew she always loved
him, even if she sometimes over-mothered him or expected
more of him than was fair for a young boy. He also blamed the
press for his mother's death.

Children who lose a parent often grow up more quickly, and
the traumatic experience distances them from their peers. Not
surprisingly, William became insular, extra-cautious about
whom he chose as a friend, and generally less trusting. Luckily
Dr Gailey, William's housemaster at Eton, gave him unwavering
support and guidance during this gruelling time.

Gradually, like most sixteen-year-olds, he began to separate
himself from his parents and think about them more objectively.
Instead, he started to focus on his own path in life. For someone
destined to be king, he would find it much more difficult, but he
was also determined to be his own man.

He knew he didn't want to live in a gilded cage, protected

from the world outside. Nor did he like anyone drawing attention to his royal status. On one occasion in his final school year when he was a member of Pop, Eton's prefects, a fellow pupil stood back to let him pass and then gave him a sweeping mock bow. William was so irritated that he swore at the boy.

What fascinated him were ordinary things his mother had gone out of her way to show him, whether it was taking his turn to see Father Christmas or getting an insight into the life of the homeless. Choosing this path was a giant leap of faith, not least because it would have to be done in public, which meant he risked the hated press making a mockery of him. He also had only a tiny amount of experience to go on. It is to his tremendous credit that he decided to give it a try. It was an experiment that could have gone disastrously wrong. He would also expend considerable energy fighting his demons, which shows how determined he was to turn from what was expected of him in the hope of saving himself from a dysfunctional future.

He also needed to get closer to his father, and fortunately an opportunity soon presented itself. The Prince of Wales would shortly be fifty, and William and Harry decided to organise a surprise birthday party for him. William was mature enough to realise his father would want Camilla to be invited, and he wisely thought it would be best to meet her privately first.

His mother had understandably thought Camilla was poison, but William wanted to make up his own mind. Unlike Diana, who involved her sons with her relationships, Charles had never introduced either of them to Camilla. William told his father he would like to see her, and a meeting was arranged for Friday, June 12, 1998 at William's self-contained flat at the top of St James's Palace, the London home of several members of the royal family.

Charles introduced them, then left them alone for about half an hour. Neither knew how the other would react and it could have been a disaster. In fact it went surprisingly easily.

William was friendly and Camilla sensitive. They met again for lunch a few days later. Subsequently, William also met her son Tom, then twenty-three, whom he liked, and her daughter Laura, then nineteen, whom both he and Harry thought was very good-looking.

Although at the time much was written about Charles being a marvellous single parent, the truth is that the boys were pretty much brought up by Tiggy or left to their own devices. Charles did though, during William's last year at Eton, get involved in the discussions about what he should do next.

Also present was William's housemaster, his former English teacher, the Commandant of Sandhurst, the Royal Military Academy, and the Bishop of London. William heard about these discussions, and insisted he have a say in the next stage of his life. He wanted a year out and to then go to St Andrews, his first choice of university, to read history of art.

William is only the second generation royal to go to university. (Prince Charles went to Cambridge.) William, however, made up his mind to be more radical and study in Scotland. He agreed to give a press interview when he arrived at university in return for being left alone during his studies, and he took the opportunity to explain his choice.

'The reason I didn't want to go to an English university is because I have lived there and wanted to get away and try somewhere else. I also knew I would be seeing a lot of Wales in the future. And I do love Scotland. There is plenty of space. I love the hills and mountains and I thought St Andrews (its oldest university) had a real community feel to it.'

In other words, he saw it as an opportunity to get as far away as possible from his family and to be left alone so he could try out how to be ordinary. It was the germ of an idea that took nerve and daring, but one that would gradually blossom to give him a fulfilled personal life. At times it was almost like being an alien in an unfamiliar world.

Part of his gap year in 2000-2001 was spent in Kenya. He was untroubled by the press and took great satisfaction in helping to build a bird hide and small cable car line across a gully at Lake Rutundu in Mount Kenya National Park. It is an isolated spot, only accessible by air, horseback, or a fifteen kilometre walk from the nearest road, and it is surrounded by elephants, hyenas, buffalo, and leopards. He chose this spot to propose to Kate Middleton in 2010.

Prince William went up to university in September 2001, feeling nervous, suspicious, and vulnerable. The university accommodates more than 8,500 students, and William chose to live in St Salvator's Hall, the smallest of the halls of residence. By the time Charles was twenty-one, he had an equerry cum private secretary, a valet, and a driver. William, who enrolled using the name William Wales, refused all offers of staff and the opportunity for somewhere exclusive to live.

Instead, he was pleased to be allocated a standard room with a shared bathroom. It was a leap into the deep end and meant he suddenly had to rely on himself to do all manner of tasks, such as buying soap, or dealing with a bank account, that he had never had to think about and that could easily have been left to an aide. It also increased the chance of fellow students selling stories about him to the media, but, in any event, the press didn't bother him at St Andrews, as they had not at Eton.

As a result, he managed to do a host of simple things, such as grocery shopping, having a drink in the pub, and eating fish and chips out of paper whilst sitting on the pavement, just like any other student. An ordinary person would find it difficult to understand how important it was for him and how it helped him feel more liberated. Despite this, he walked about wearing a baseball cap to partially hide his face and kept his eyes fixed downward to avoid being accosted by a stranger. Nor did he yet feel able to trust anyone.

He had, though, begun chatting casually with a girl called

Kate Middleton, who had a room close to his in the same hall and was also studying history of art. William and Kate met regularly, walking to and from the halls of residence and lectures, and began slowly building up a friendship. They played tennis and drank in local bars. She was confident and pretty and made him laugh. What particularly appealed to him was that she was obviously middle-class. Kate admitted during the interview she and William gave to the media following their engagement that initially she found it very difficult to talk to the future heir to the crown. 'I actually think I went bright red when I met you and sort of scuttled off,' she said, smiling at her new fiancé. They also discovered that she, like him, had worked as a volunteer abroad during her gap year.

William's interest in her wasn't merely friendly. In 2002, he paid £200 for a front-row seat to watch her sashay down an improvised catwalk in the Students' Union nearly naked in a see-through black lace dress over a black bra and bikini bottom. It was a student-organised event to raise funds for charity. She may have had an element of calculation in her modelling. It certainly did the trick with William, and the picture of her has since become iconic.

The following March, William suffered an emotional setback. He, Harry, and some friends were skiing with Prince Charles in Klosters, Switzerland, when they received the news that Queen Elizabeth the Queen Mother, aged 101, had died peacefully in her sleep at Royal Lodge, Windsor. Her daughter the Queen was by her side. The royal party returned home and William, along with Harry and other members of the royal family, walked behind her coffin at the state funeral in Westminster Abbey. It must have triggered agonising memories of his mother's funeral, but once again he was required to keep his emotions under tight control.

The event disturbed his composure. In common with many students, he began to go through a difficult patch towards the end of his first academic year. He felt increasingly homesick and felt he wanted to leave university. He was also weary of the endless effort it took to try to be ordinary and one of the boys, when his future meant he was patently not. He discussed the matter in general with his father and grandfather and both urged him to stay. His grandfather didn't like a quitter and made the point forcefully.

He also sought advice from his former Eton housemaster and, perhaps to his own surprise, from Kate Middleton, who has been given the credit for persuading him to stay. After careful thought, he decided instead of leaving he would change his course to geography. By the time he returned in September 2002, he felt confident enough to share £400-a-week digs with Kate and two other friends. It was another normal thing to do, but one that would give him a much-needed chance to quietly observe and learn how people lived together. Were, for example, yelling matches, tears, and bitter silences normal behaviour, or were his parents the exception? He had managed to negotiate his first year; living with a small group of friends would take him on to the next stage on his personal road to redemption and a more stable future.

Life was obviously harmonious, as by the end of their second year he and Kate had begun a relationship. 'It just blossomed', he admitted coyly at the engagement interview. The following year, they and their two housemates moved to a secluded stone cottage with open fires at the end of a pot-holed farm track in open countryside, well away from prying eyes. Kate was by now mothering William and cooking him dinner most evenings. 'He basically couldn't live without her,' said one friend. Her maternal style was even in evidence on their wedding day and has been ever since.

Living as an ordinary student with an ordinary girlfriend of whom William was becoming increasingly fond had the potential of gradually breaking down the web of destruction he had inherited. But it required continual effort not to fall back on the patterns of his past. It's not easy to change hard-wired habits that have been passed down through several generations, and it takes strong commitment to stay on track and bit by bit get rid of old habits. It became William's life plan, along with his acceptance of his destiny to be king.

# *Seven*
# The middle class Middletons

IT IS NOT KNOWN EXACTLY WHEN KATE FIRST TOOK HER BOY-
FRIEND home to meet her family, who then lived in a five-bed-
room house in Bucklebury, West Berkshire, but it seems everyone got on well from the start. William made a point of speaking
fondly of the Middletons during the engagement interview.
'Kate's got a very, very close family. Mike and Carole have been
really loving and caring and really fun and have been really wel-
coming towards me so I've felt really a part of the family'. Many
young men have no problem meeting their girlfriends' parents,
particularly at the age of twenty, when commitment and marriage remain far in the future. But it was another extraordinarily
brave step for William to take. The Middletons could have made
him feel apart and awkward, or been too reverential towards
him, either of which might have spoilt what he had with Kate.

Instead, Kate's parents' normal background and the fact that
she was, unlike him, the product of a loving, stable home enhanced her appeal. His parents' marriage had been turbulent
and he must often have wondered if, behind closed doors, most
people lived this way. Here at last was an opportunity to find
out what ordinary family life was all about. He couldn't afford
to miss it.

Kate's father, Michael, was born in Leeds, Yorkshire, the son
of an airline pilot. He became a steward with British Airways in

the mid-1970s, when he met and fell in love with Carole Gold-smith, an air hostess. She was a builder's daughter, descended from a family of Durham coal miners, was brought up in a municipal flat in Southall, a nondescript West London suburb, and went to the local state school.

Michael and Carole married in June 1980. Kate, or Catherine as the family call her, and the name by which William has said she should be known, was born at the Royal Berkshire Hospital in Reading on January 9, 1982. A second daughter, Philippa, known as Pippa, arrived in 1983, and a boy, James, was born in 1987.

Kate was born under the astrological sign of Capricorn. Capricorn women want to succeed and are down-to-earth, self-motivated, patient, and responsible. They often find it difficult to express their emotions and are naturally cautious. Capricorn women place a high value on material security, and are difficult to get to know. They can be pessimistic and fear failure, but most of all, they enjoy setting long-term goals and going after them until they succeed.

The two sisters are close, and Pippa has admitted that the family is fiercely competitive. While young Kate had to work hard and is more solitary, Pippa is naturally sporty and more gregarious, and found everything easy.

As a little girl, Kate loved dressing up as a clown in baggy dungarees and playing musical statues. Once Kate and Pippa were at preschool, Carole Middleton, by far the more ambitious of the couple, set up Party Pieces, a company which began by making party bags but grew to sell a variety of party goods by mail order and subsequently online. The business was hugely successful and her husband joined her. Michael and Carole sent all their children to private schools. Their first choice for Kate was Downe House, Berkshire, where she was bullied. She persuaded her parents to take her away, and when she was fourteen, they sent her to Marlborough College in Wiltshire, an exclusive coeducational boarding school founded in 1843.

At first she felt homesick and cried herself to sleep at night. A group of sixth-form boys initially gave her one or two points out of ten for her looks. But the shy young girl blossomed in the sixth form and was particularly good at sport. She played hockey for the school and was captain of the tennis team.

Described as 'a goody two shoes', she had no interest in rebelling and, unlike Diana, was level-headed and always in control of herself. Perhaps her only idiosyncrasy was that she enjoyed microwaving Marmite sandwiches. Kate left school with excellent academic results – eleven GCSEs and three A Levels – but apparently said she 'wanted to get married, have loads of children, live in a farmhouse in the middle of nowhere, have lots of horses and go skiing'.

Many mothers cherish ambitions for their daughters to marry good-looking, rich young men to keep them in the manner to which they could soon become accustomed. To have a prince as a son-in-law must be beyond most mothers' dreams. Ironically, while William has sought to embrace a family lifestyle several rungs down on the social ladder, the Middletons have seized their chance to rise and since the royal wedding have jumped to the top of every guest list.

They bought a London flat in Chelsea, which Kate lived in after university and which Pippa and James subsequently shared, and they extended their house in Bucklebury. Carole Middleton also promoted her party firm's baby shower collection just before Kate's due date for Prince George.

It hasn't, however, been a completely free ride for the family. Carole, James and Pippa have all been accused of using Kate's position to promote their business interests. Carole has been mocked over her past and nicknamed 'Doors to Manual', a reference to her former job as an air hostess. She has been accused of some nifty calculating of her own by sending Kate to St Andrews in the hope that she and William would meet. She also faced criticism for a monster faux pas – chewing gum (it was later revealed to be of the nicotine variety) at William's passing-out parade from the Royal Military Academy at Sandhurst in 2006. Pippa and James have been criticised for a variety of reasons including sitting in a prominent position in the Royal Box at the Wimbledon tennis championships, as the much-sought-after places are generally given to those who have made a significant contribution to society and are traditionally filled with celebrities, senior politicians and sportsmen.

Pippa has also been accused of trying to upstage Kate both at the royal wedding and Charlotte's baptism and of capitalising on her royal connection to advance her career. Despite endless opportunities, many of her projects have failed. She was given a £400,000 advance by Penguin Books to write a party book, *Celebrate!* – it was ridiculed and sold poorly. She was asked to write a column for Waitrose Kitchen, which launched in April 2013 and was fiercely criticised for its banality. Undaunted, she agreed to write a column for the Daily Telegraph. This was quietly dropped after six months.

She also became a contributing editor at Vanity Fair magazine. Her pieces were laughed at for stating the obvious. Her attempt to move into TV and work for NBC failed to get off the ground. James Middleton was condemned for insensitivity when he used a picture of Princess Diana on one of 21 cakes he made for a feature to celebrate Hello! magazine's birthday. His latest business, Boomf, makes personalised marshmallows.

William, however, is very protective of Kate's immediate family. He no doubt realises that they may sometimes have taken commercial advantage of their royal connection, but if their knuckles have been rapped as has happened to other royal inlaws in the past, nothing has leaked in public. Far more important to William is that they have given him the chance to experience how a warm, stable family lives. He particularly enjoys Carole and Michael's company and has gone on holiday with them to the Caribbean island of Mustique, watched television at their home with supper on his lap, and, so it is alleged, calls Kate's father 'Dad'.

William's unique relationship with his in-laws has also undoubtedly helped liberate him from his past. Significantly, his interest in middle-class families hasn't extended to anyone else he has met. There is little doubt that the amount of time William has chosen to spend with the Middletons shows that a normal, middle-class, close and loving family is just what he would have wanted his own to be like. He has relished the feeling of security, comfort and protection it has given him. For the first time since his troubled childhood, he finally had the opportunity to begin to heal. He didn't have to worry about what he said. He wasn't expected to be responsible for how anyone felt or find solutions to their emotional problems. There was no pressure. He felt accepted for himself.

They have become so close that Carole and Michael even moved into special quarters in an annex of Amner Hall for several weeks to help run the couple's country residence. Carole organised the household while Michael is believed to have kept an eye on the gardeners. They helped Kate employ a new housekeeper and subsequently prepare for the arrival of her second child. Carole, who is highly organised, still finds time to run her business.

In return, William has insisted that the Middletons be treated well by the royal family, which has set another precedent. The Queen and Prince Philip have notoriously ignored in-laws, including the Spencers, failing to invite them to anything. They have made an exception for the Middletons, who were even asked to join the Queen, despite the absence of Kate and William, to watch the racing at Royal Ascot in 2012. They were also allowed to be part of the official photographs following both christenings. Not everyone approves of them. It is rumoured that if Charles and Camilla had their way, they wouldn't give the

Middletons house room, but they are courteous to them because it is what William demands. Because of his difficult childhood, no one wants to offend him.

William invited Kate to his twenty-first birthday party, organised by Prince Charles and the Queen at Windsor Castle, for 300 family members and friends. The theme was 'Out of Africa'. He subsequently made sure she didn't take the relationship seriously by insisting, during an interview to mark the occasion, that he didn't have a steady girlfriend.

William next faced the hurdle of coping with his late mother's former butler, Paul Burrell. Burrell produced a letter he claimed Princess Diana had written suggesting that Prince Charles was planning a fatal car crash so that he would be free to marry Camilla. Burrell was effectively calling Charles a murderer.

William was livid. He spoke to Harry, who was on his gap year in Australia, and they issued a joint press release. The statement included the words, 'We cannot believe that Paul, who was entrusted with so much, could abuse his position in such a cold and overt betrayal.' Yet another person had let William down, but fortunately it didn't seem to hold him back for long.

William and Kate's romance was eventually exposed when she was spotted with him on the ski slopes at Klosters in March 2004. He subsequently again made the point in public that he was not thinking of settling down. 'Look, I'm only twenty-two, for God's sake,' he stated. 'I am too young to marry at my age. I don't want to get married until I am at least 28 or 30.' His statement highlighted the battle that he was waging. Emotionally he wanted to be with her, but he was scared of commitment. Other girls, particularly if they, like Kate, longed for marriage and children, might have quit. Kate was prepared to wait forever – and nearly had to.

By his fourth and final year at St Andrews, William had obviously made strides both socially and personally, and was popular and respected. Dr Charles Warren, a lecturer at the university, told the author Penny Junor that he found William remarkably humble.

'I formed a very high opinion of him as a man with his feet on the ground, earthed and normal, always a pleasure to deal with and interact with. He had no sense of entitlement, was never pushy. He was an outstanding young man by any standards by the fact that he's had all that privilege and extraordinary life, yet he was most normal. Whoever the people were that had a hand in bringing him up, they deserve a lot of credit.'

William had worked hard on himself to come across as normal and unpretentious. He had ongoing issues, but his next great challenge was to deal with other aspects of his damaged childhood, especially trusting others and overcoming his fear of being abandoned.

Both he and Kate left university with sound 2:1 degrees. Kate got a job as an accessory buyer for the fashion chain Jigsaw. William wanted a military career and was accepted at the Royal Military Academy, Sandhurst, in 2006, graduating that December. Kate attended his passing-out parade, the first time she had been seen at a high-profile event at which the Queen and other senior royals were present.

William subsequently moved to an army camp in Dorset to serve with the Blues and Royals. Kate stayed in London. Working in different parts of the country meant they could no longer see each other every day, an absence that did not make William's heart grow fonder. Sometimes when he came up to London he chose to go clubbing with friends rather than see her. They had been together for five years, since they were twenty, and William's thoughts strayed to relationships with other women. He reportedly complained he was finding the relationship 'confining' and 'claustrophobic'.

Over the previous four years, William had spent part of each Easter break with the Middletons, but that year he declined their invitation without giving an explanation. It was a particularly difficult time for Kate. Without William by her side, as a mere girlfriend she was not entitled to royal protection to shield her from the paparazzi. Lawyers had, on her behalf, asked the press to leave her alone, but they didn't take much notice. She was left to deal on her own with a continual scrum of reporters and photographers, plus curious members of the public, and at times it was scary. She talked about her concerns with William, perhaps unaware it would trigger traumatic memories of his mother. It was an opportunity to propose. Instead he ended the relationship in a phone call to her at the office.

He reportedly told her, 'The press will make your life unbearable as long as we're together. I don't want you suffering the way my mother did. It just isn't going to work. It isn't fair to you.' Life together had been simple to arrange in the cocoon that university provided. Now that they were living apart from each other, the relationship needed more effort, and he was scared. He had had too much responsibility for his mother's happiness, and it seemed too daunting to take on being responsible for Kate.

Kate was miserable too, but no doubt following the advice of her mother and sister, instead of sitting moping at home she hit the town night after night with a brave face and very sexy dresses. The clothes weren't her usual style and were perhaps borrowed from Pippa. She also subtly showed William that she could look after herself and, more importantly, cope with her own emotions. William quickly realised he couldn't bear her to be with another man and within three months they were back together. During the engagement interview, Kate gave what sounded like a prepared, upbeat answer to the inevitable question about what went wrong. 'At the time I don't think I was very happy about it,' she said. 'But actually it made me a stronger person.'

Love, of course, isn't about ticking a wish list or an intellectual analysis of pros and cons, and many young men find it difficult to make a lifetime commitment to a woman. The combination of his turbulent background and being second in line to the throne made William's position much harder, and he kept getting cold feet. He wouldn't be ready to commit for another three and a half years, but his major wobble had several positive outcomes. He accepted he had deep feelings for Kate and felt at ease with her family. She'd also shown that, despite suffering a certain humiliation when he ended their relationship, she neither abandoned him nor sold the story of their romance. Instead she had behaved with considerable dignity and shown how solid, reliable, and caring she was.

They knew each other well and she had never betrayed his trust. She also had not put a foot wrong with members of the press, even though they called her 'Waity Katie' and implied that all she was doing with her life was waiting for William to propose. Nor had she put William under pressure.

Outweighing the positive were traits common to those who come from a dysfunctional family. Psychological patterns, just like physical illnesses, resurface generation after generation, and children who, like William, take on a parent-like role when they are young, find it difficult to trust, not just others but their own judgment and actions. They also fear abandonment, block feelings so they are not hurt again, and lack a belief that they can change their destiny. It was a real battle for William, who confessed in the engagement interview that he was a 'real romantic', but one he eventually, after a great deal of soul-searching and consistent effort, proved he could win.

Soon after their rapprochement, Kate was a VIP guest in the royal box at the memorial concert William and Harry put on to mark the tenth anniversary of Diana's death. It was also the first occasion on which the two brothers spoke publicly about their loss. Talking to Fearne Cotton for the BBC and to a journalist from NBC's 'Today' programme, William said:

'We were left in no doubt that we were the most important thing in her life and then after that there was everyone else, there were all her charities and everything like that and, to me, that's a really good philosophy – she just loved caring for people and she loved helping. We were so lucky to have her as our mother and there's not a day that goes past when we don't think about her and miss her influence, because she was a massive example to both of us. It's one of those things that is very sad but you learn to deal with it and there are plenty of other people out there who have got the same or worse problems than we've had.'

The concert, which 63,000 people attended, took the princes seven months to organise and took place at the new Wembley Stadium on July 1, 2007. The concert was also broadcast in 140 countries and raised £1million for the Diana Memorial Fund and five charities. The performers included dancers from the English National Ballet, Kiefer Sutherland, Ricky Gervais, Jamie Oliver, and David Beckham, plus video recordings from Nelson Mandela, Bill Clinton, and Tony Blair. To avoid upsetting their father, the Queen, or Prince Philip, who were still sensitive about anything to do with their mother, they did not invite any members of the royal family.

William thanked everyone at the end of the concert, saying 'Thank you to all of you who have come here tonight to celebrate our mother's life. For us this has been the most perfect way to remember her, and this is how she would want to be remembered'.

# *Eight*
# Kate passes the test

In 2009, William decided to transfer to the RAF and train to be a helicopter pilot with the RAF's Search and Rescue Force, based in Anglesey, an island off the northwest coast of Wales. It was a good omen, as Anglesey is the resting place of Saint Dwynwen, the Welsh Saint Valentine and patron saint of lovers. William was subsequently involved with dozens of rescue missions, plucking individuals out of icy water and winching them to safety. Flight Lieutenant William Wales, as he was known in the RAF, loved the work and said in a BBC Wales documentary, 'Helicopter Rescue', in April 2013, 'There's no greater feeling than when you've actually done some good and saved someone's life'.

At first, he lived on his own in a rented farmhouse, practising those ordinary things he came to enjoy, such as shopping and cooking. Kate initially came for short visits but later moved in. When William wasn't working, they lived a very quiet and solitary existence away from the press, the public, and the razzmatazz of a royal life. It was just the two of them and nature. Living together away from others would put their relationship to a final test.

They had displayed their best selves during their very long courtship, but now they had no escape from seeing every last flaw in each other's characters. Would Kate really be happy with what she saw in him? He also had the opportunity to let himself become really close to her. As time evolved and the relationship survived, he slowly built up his confidence to ask her to marry him and silence any remaining negative thoughts in his head about trust and commitment. William finally proposed in October 2010 during a holiday in Kenya. It took Kate by surprise, or at least she pretended it did. It was a hammer blow to his dysfunctional past.

At the engagement interview, where they were both obviously very nervous, he said, 'We've talked about it (marriage) lots. So it's always been something we've had a good chat about and ... both of us have come to the decision pretty much together. I just chose when to do it and how to do it – and obviously being a real romantic, I did it extremely well'!

He said he also wanted to give her time 'to back out if she needed to before it all got too much', adding significantly, 'I have wanted to try to learn from lessons in the past'.

He confessed that he had carried his mother's sapphire and diamond £28,500 engagement ring in his rucksack for three weeks before proposing. 'Because I planned it, it went fine', he smiled. 'You hear a lot of horror stories about proposing and things going horribly wrong – it went really, really well and I was really pleased she said "Yes". We've been talking about it for a long time, so for us, it's a real relief, and it's really nice to be able to tell everybody'. He chose his mother's ring as a 'way of keeping her close by'.

The interview revealed touching aspects of his character, particularly his feeling that Kate might, in the end, have turned him down. It was why, he said, he wanted to ask her before checking that it was okay with her father. Getting engaged is a pivotal moment for anyone. For William, it was overpowering. He had won his battle to trust his emotions and find fulfilment. He felt secure that Kate wanted him, and had found his emotional place in the world. From that the rest would come. Most importantly, he wasn't going to have a dysfunctional relationship like his parents.

The Queen has always monitored the actions of her close family when it comes to choosing a marital partner. Kate's presence, however, coincided with her accepting that, as three out of her four children, Prince Charles, Prince Andrew, and Princess Anne, had failed marriages, she was a poor matchmaker. As a result, she decided to take a back seat as far as all her grandchildren were concerned, despite the fact that William is a future king.

Queen Elizabeth the Queen Mother or the Queen's sister Princess Margaret might well have had a quiet word in her ear to ask if she really thought someone whose family was 'in trade' was the right kind of person to be marrying into the royal family, but both had passed away. The Queen was also shrewd enough to recognise that the public liked Kate, which was good news for the future of the royal family.

As befits a modern couple, the news broke first on Twitter, and then went viral. The tweet read: 'The Prince of Wales is delighted to announce the engagement of Prince William to Miss Catherine Middleton.'

Becoming engaged to the second in line to the throne instantly made Kate a public figure, entitled to royal protection in her own right. William insisted that she, unlike his mother, be given every help in performing her royal duties; he would not let her suffer from the press as his mother had done, or allow any invasion of their privacy.

Initially he was not so successful guarding her privacy. The paparazzi photographed a topless Kate during the 2012 Diamond Jubilee tour of the South Seas, and again when she wore a blue bikini when pregnant while on a private holiday with him in Mustique. While the topless photographs were a total invasion of her privacy, it is perhaps also risky to go topless anywhere when you are married to a senior royal.

The royal wedding was booked for Friday April 29, 2011 at

Westminster Abbey, and both bride and groom were determined that they wanted, as far as was feasible, what William called 'a personal day...we want a day that is as enjoyable as possible, for as many people as possible'.

The first obstacle came almost immediately after their engagement was announced. The Lord Chamberlain recommended a list of 777 names who, according to protocol, should be invited. This was hardly what William wanted. He told Robert Hardman, who was writing a biography of the Queen, what happened next. 'I rang her (The Queen) up the next day and said, 'Do we need to be doing this'? And she said, 'No. Start with your friends first and then go from there'. She made the point that there are certain times when you have to strike the right balance (between personal and duty). And it's advice like that, which is really key, when you know that she's seen and done it before.'

He often bypassed staff involved in the planning and instead visited the Queen for about half an hour each week to sort out the details of both ceremony and celebration. William and Kate's personal touches included setting up a royal gift fund. They asked guests to make a donation to one of twenty-six little-known charities they had chosen together rather than give them any presents. Their gesture raised over £1 million.

The night before the wedding took place, when most grooms are calming their nerves or finishing their speeches, William and Harry emerged from Clarence House, the Queen Mother's former home, to talk to some of the thousands of people lining the pavements. Many people, of all types and ages, had arrived days previously with sleeping bags, balloons, silly hats, and champagne to grab a good spot to watch the proceedings. 'You're amazing', William beamed as he shook countless hands. 'These crowds are amazing. Thank you so much'. The warmth and palpable support from the crowds must have helped him banish any last-minute nerves.

The wedding itself was a perfect combination of pomp and

intimacy, state and private. Many who lined the route could be seen brushing away a tear, and it was certainly not the day to be a cynic or a republican. The crowds cheered and waved at the young couple who had finally and publicly sealed their love. Several of those interviewed spoke about William's tough childhood, how pleased they were he had finally made up his mind to marry his Kate, and that his mother would have been so proud.

Kate, now to be known as Her Royal Highness, the Duchess of Cambridge, didn't stop beaming. Although she hadn't agreed to obey in the formal service, she remains in thrall to William, who is the dominant partner in the relationship. She also indicated by the same subtle gesture throughout the emotional day – both in the 1902 State Landau that took the couple from the ceremony at Westminster Abbey to Buckingham Palace and on the Palace balcony – that William would be well looked after and that she had his interests at heart.

In the car, she slightly jolted her body as if she had suddenly seen something, pointed towards it, then leant towards him to say something that invariably made him smile. It was reminiscent of the sort of behaviour a mother might display when showing something of interest to her loved child.

William, the little boy who had had to assume a parental role and had taken on the responsibility for the well-being of his mother, had finally broken through. He had married at the age he wanted to, to the woman he and no one else had chosen. He had test-run the relationship for so long that they knew each other intimately and had built up a close understanding. He had worked hard on himself and tried to be brave; now it had paid off. He had seen how a bad marriage could really undo a person; his, he felt, would be the making of him. He had escaped from his past.

The newlyweds honeymooned in the Seychelles. William then went back to work as a search and rescue pilot while Kate, who has willingly accommodated her life to him and whose friends are his, did their shopping in the local supermarket, cooked his meals, and ran his bath.

Her first full-on experience of royal duty was accompanying her husband on an official ten-day tour of Canada, two months after the wedding. William and Harry had visited Canada a year after their mother's death; if returning there awakened complex memories, he now had someone close to share them with. The tour was a tremendous success. Kate behaved as if she was having the best time of her life, and talked easily to strangers and children.

An insider has said that she is not a natural hugger, like Diana, and had to be encouraged to get down to talk to children. Her reticence may well be because she is still on the steep learning curve of how to be a senior royal. The couple visited seven cities in five provinces, and it was obvious from their rapturous reception that the Diana factor had been replaced by the Kate Middleton factor. William, unlike his father, seemed genuinely thrilled that his new wife had wowed the crowds, even though he has told friends he does not want her to become a people's princess like his mother and would prefer her to retain a more traditional royal air of mystery.

He even experienced some very un-royal moments when his feelings overwhelmed him and he gave her a hug. It is an ordinary enough gesture for a new husband to make, but here at last was a sign that he didn't mind showing his feelings. He is unlikely, however, to become either an extrovert or gregarious, and even maintains a distance from other members of the royal family. Although William and Kate occasionally see Zara and Peter Phillips, Princess Anne's children, they are not close to Prince Andrew's daughters, Princesses Beatrice and Eugenie, and barely see the royal aunts or uncles.

Kate has performed royal duties on her own while William worked in Anglesey. She was by his side in 2012 during the Queen's Jubilee celebrations, at the London Olympics, and when he represented the Queen during a hugely successful nine-day tour of southeast Asia and the South Pacific. Those same gestures and quick asides seen at their wedding again connected them throughout these events and made each experience a shared one.

Couples who have been together for a long time before getting married often want children as soon as possible. William and Kate perhaps decided to wait until after the Jubilee and Olympics to avoid diverting attention from these unique events onto themselves, but they wasted no time once the events were over. The news became public before they had intended when Kate was hospitalised, suffering from an acute form of morning sickness, at the beginning of December 2012.

The increasingly confident William put Kate's welfare, and perhaps his own wish, before royal tradition. Instead of the customary royal Christmas with the Queen and other members of the royal family at Sandringham, he chose to spend the day privately with the Middleton family at home in Bucklebury, sharing an ordinary, albeit increasingly upwardly mobile, family's festivities. The press were barred from taking any photographs of the Middletons going to church.

# *Nine*
# A new heir and a healing process

KATE'S LAST PUBLIC APPEARANCE BEFORE THE ROYAL BIRTH WAS ON June 15, 2013. She was eight months pregnant and joined the rest of the royal family for the Trooping the Colour military parade which celebrated the 87-year-old Queen's official birthday.

The Duchess looked well in the latter stages of her pregnancy. Her choice to wear a baby pink outfit with matching hat, by designer Alexander McQueen, sparked rumours that she was having a girl. In fact, Kate and William had chosen not to discover the sex of their baby before it was born.

Princess Diana made one of her most significant breaks with convention by insisting that Prince William would be born in hospital rather than in Buckingham Palace. It was the first time this had happened with an heir to the throne. Kate, as she has done many times since her engagement to William in November 2010, followed in Diana's footsteps and planned to give birth in the private Lindo Wing of St Mary's Hospital, west London. It remains very important to William to connect wherever possible to his late mother and anything that is important to William is equally important to Kate. Kate had reportedly also asked her mother and sister to be on call for the baby's birth in case William didn't make it in time from his work as a rescue pilot in Anglesey. The Queen thoughtfully put a 175mph maroon Sikorsky-S76c high-speed helicopter of the Queen's Flight on standby at RAF Northolt, west London, to whisk William to Kate's bedside once she was in labour. The pilot would make a 600-mile trip to get him to his wife's side in four hours.

In the event, none of this was needed. Prince William drove Kate the short distance to the hospital from their Kensington Palace home. Almost from the moment when Kate retreated from public view with one month to go, media excitement and anticipation moved into top gear. Television crews, reporters, photographers and well-wishers took up residence outside the hospital. Metal ladders, placed to get the best view of the door of the Lindo Wing for the key picture of mother, father and child, formed a mountainous ridge along the pavement. Most royal occasions are planned meticulously in advance with precision timing, but of course babies have a timetable of their own and often place scant regard to the impatience of the waiting world.

The wait seemed interminable and, with no sign of an early arrival, the media began to run out of things to say – except to interview each other – about the fact that nothing was happening. Baby supplements were prepared and then dropped. On July 20 the Daily Mail cheekily published a 'Royal Baby Album: a gorgeous souvenir to celebrate Kate and William's new arrival.' The arrival was still two long days away. Editors commissioned polls to fill columns about the birth. One Ipsos Mori Poll reported that 65 per cent of the public would like the royal child to have a proper paid job before taking on royal duties full time. Another poll reported that three out of ten people wanted the child to go to a state school.

The royals couldn't keep their excitement and concern under wraps either. Camilla let slip during a visit to a children's hospice near St Austell, Cornwall, on July 15 that she and Prince Charles were 'just waiting by the telephone. We are hopeful that by the end of the week he or she will be here.' Even the Queen, usually so reticent, revealed her hope that 'he or she would hurry up', as she was about to go off for the summer to Balmoral. There were even rumours that the media were waiting outside the wrong hospital. Meanwhile, Kate and William relocated to the Middletons' family home in the village of Bucklebury, Berkshire, for what was to be the last week that they would be merely a couple. It provided a much-needed haven where they could relax and spend special time together before becoming parents.

Two days before the birth, they moved to Kensington Palace. Then, in the early hours of Monday July 22, a day they will surely talk about with nostalgia all their lives, Kate went into labour. At 5.30 am, as thunder rumbled across the sky, she and William arrived at the side door of the Lindo Wing unseen by anyone except a couple of freelance photographers. They were soon settled in a birthing suite.

The announcement for which billions of people round the world had been waiting with growing anxiety finally came at 8.30 pm on July 22. The former Kate Middleton, a young woman from an ordinary family but now Duchess of Cambridge and the wife to the second in line to the British throne, had given birth to a healthy baby boy, prince and future king at 4.24pm after a labour lasting at least ten hours on the hottest day of the year. The baby weighed a solid 8 pounds 6 ounces, making him the heaviest future monarch in a hundred years. He was considerably bigger than his father, Prince William, who had weighed a mere 7 pounds 1 ounce. William immediately telephoned the Queen, Prince Charles, Prince Harry and Kate's parents. Prince George, by the way, is a Cancerian like his father and his grandmother Diana, Princess of Wales, forging perhaps a special astrological link with both.

William then waited four hours before giving the go-ahead for the birth to be made public. Announcing the arrival of the royal baby had initially posed a challenge for the royal couple in this multimedia age. Should it be announced first on Twitter? Would William want to make the announcement himself from the steps of the hospital? It was reported that Kate and

William decided to respect the stately tradition and protocol of royal births and have the announcement first posted outside Buckingham Palace.

In the end, however, the couple announced the birth by posting it on their Royal Highnesses' official website and in a press release by email from Kensington Palace. It noted that William was present at the birth and was 'delighted.' No wonder. The birth of an heir to the throne is a rare and special event, full of historical significance as well as personal joy. But it is also the most intimate time in a couple's life. Creating a new life signifies a new beginning. Neither Kate nor William will ever be quite the same again. For Kate, as for most women, the arrival of a first child is undoubtedly one of the most exciting things that can happen. For William the emotion he must have felt that at last he had his own family would be overwhelming. There would have been huge relief for the safe delivery of his son and unconditional love and an intense desire to protect both his tiny baby, so vulnerable and precious, and the woman who has given him something more valuable than The Crown Jewels.

There must also have been profound sadness too that his late mother wasn't there to share his happiness and would never meet or enjoy her grandson. On the other hand, his new status as a father was also the surest way to exorcise his troubled years. He now had a chance to give the child stability and love and be the sort of father he had wanted for himself. William has grown up knowing he had to keep his feelings under wraps. He trusted few people and only reluctantly learnt to live in the spotlight. Kate's devotion, confidence and love had helped him trust his feelings. Now his son would be the perfect catalyst to allow him to find even greater personal happiness and the inner confidence to make his own choices.

The four-hour period between the birth and the official announcement gave him the opportunity to spend irreplaceable time with Kate and their baby. It was no surprise to learn that

William chose to stay with Kate and his child in the hospital and hold on to those early moments. The public and media would have to wait. Instead of emerging on to the hospital steps to address the serried ranks of media crews he sent out a short message. 'We couldn't be happier,' it read. It was a sign not just of his total commitment to his wife and new-born child but also an acknowledgement that he understands what is truly important in his life. He promises to be a very different father from Prince Charles, leaning instead to his mother's more emotional approach. It will no doubt make him a more balanced king.

When the rumour spread that the baby had arrived the crowds erupted into cheers and hordes rushed to the gate of Buckingham Palace. Minutes later, a member of the royal household appeared at the front door of the Lindo Wing, at the time the most watched front door in the world, his head down but with a smile on his face, to pass a folder containing details of the birth to a waiting driver who whisked it the short distance to Buckingham Palace. The announcement was quickly framed and Philip Rhodes, senior page at St James's Palace, was given the honour of carrying it to be set on the gold-painted tripod, used to announce the birth of Prince William, at the gates of Buckingham Palace.

The announcement was brief to the point of being terse. 'Her Royal Highness, the Duchess of Cambridge, was safely delivered of a son at 4.24 pm. Her Royal Highness and the child are both doing well.' It was signed by the Queen's former gynaecologist Marcus Setchell and two other members of the medical team that had helped deliver the baby.

Somehow this bit of formal flummery seemed a side show. It was fortunate perhaps that Kate and William didn't have to consider another royal tradition, that of having a cabinet minister – usually the Home Secretary – in attendance to act as witness and ensure that the baby was not swapped with another child. This practice, which began in the 17th century, was stopped by the

Queen's father, King George VI, shortly before Prince Charles
was born in 1948. In the past the Foreign Office was responsible for notifying the UK's overseas territories while Buckingham
Palace has directly contacted all the Commonwealth realms
with the news of a royal birth. By the time Prince Charles was
born in 1948 the news was immediately broadcast on the BBC
with the announcer stating: 'Listeners will want us to offer their
loyal congratulations to Princess Elizabeth and the Royal Family
on this happy occasion.'

Not long after the new prince's birth the City of London, the
London Eye and the fountain around Nelson's column in Tra-
falgar Square were lit up in variations of red, white and especially blue. Jubilant crowds cheered and waved even though no
member of the royal family had appeared. Congratulations from
home and abroad poured in thick and fast.

The baby's arrival also meant that Kate's mother was elevat-
ed to the country's most influential granny. Carole and Michael
Middleton were the first to meet the baby prince, two hours
ahead of Prince Charles and Camilla, Duchess of Cornwall,
which marked another break with protocol. Prince Charles
could barely conceal his happiness – and no doubt relief – that
the waiting was over. 'Both my wife and I are overjoyed at the
arrival of my first grandchild,' he said. 'It is an incredibly special moment for William and Catherine and we are so thrilled
for them on the birth of their baby boy. Grandparenthood is a
unique moment in anyone's life as countless kind people have
told me in recent months. So I am enormously proud and happy
to be a grandfather for the first time. And we are eagerly looking
forward to seeing the baby in the near future.'

The Queen and Prince Philip announced their delight. For
the Queen, the news brought two types of happiness: first, the
pleasure of a great-grandson, and second, the confidence that
the monarchy was secure for three generations to come. The
Prime Minister, David Cameron, described the news as 'an his-

toric moment in the life of our nation' but added that 'above all it's a wonderful moment for a warm and loving couple who have got a new baby boy.' President Barack Obama and his wife sent their good wishes: 'Michelle and I are so pleased to congratulate the Duke and Duchess of Cambridge on the joyous occasion of the birth of their first child. We wish them all the happiness and blessings parenthood brings. The child enters the world at a time of promise and opportunity for our two nations. Given the special relationship between us, the American people are pleased to join with the people of the United Kingdom as they celebrate the birth of the young prince.'

As for Twitter, it went into viral meltdown, with everyone from celebrities to ordinary members of the public united in tweeting their excitement and relief. Even before the baby's birth 487 million users had viewed posts about the Duchess of Cambridge and within four hours of the birth 500,000 tweets had been sent mentioning the new prince.

Prince Willliam stayed overnight in the hospital. The following day Kate cautiously descended the steps from the Lindo Wing to return to Kensington Palace. She looked radiant in a lilac purple dress by British designer Jenny Packham, which she teamed with her favourite cream wedges. Her hair fell in waves around her face and she was meticulously made up. She handed William their baby, carefully wrapped up in a hand-knitted fine lace white shawl. The expression on William's face as he gazed down at his new-born son was one of tenderness and joy.

It was to be just a quick photocall but one Kate used to reveal that William had already changed his first nappy. 'I did the first nappy, it's a badge of honor,' he later explained. It is inconceivable that any previous heir to the throne would have even contemplated doing such a thing

They came out again shortly afterwards. William was carrying his precious cargo in a car seat and faced the practical hurdle of fitting it into the back of the car. Prince Charles, who expects a servant to put toothpaste on his toothbrush when he wants to clean his teeth, would have been aghast, but William's determination to 'keep grounded' meant he was going to do it himself. Despite admitting to practising beforehand it was still a struggle and brave to undertake such a tricky manoeuvre while the world watched. He then proudly drove his wife and baby son home. Later, in an interview with American TV station CNN, he said: 'I think driving your son and your wife away from hospital was really important to me. I had to practise [installing the car seat], I really did – I was terrified it was going to fall off or the door wasn't going to close properly.'

The following day it was announced that the baby prince would be named George Alexander Louis and that he would be formally known as Prince George of Cambridge. The infant, who is third in line to the throne, immediately replaced Prince Harry, who dropped to fourth place, while Andrew, Prince Charles's brother, dropped to fifth. The fact that the child was a boy also rendered academic all the discussion and negotiations that had taken place of the constitutional changes in recognising a baby girl as the next in line to the throne after William.

Unlike his father, who expects to be surrounded by staff, Prince William had several years previously dispensed with flunkies, maids, footmen and valets. Following George's birth Palace officials confirmed that the couple would not have a nanny and instead would rely upon their families' help, stating: 'They have both got families that will care hugely for this baby.' This proved to be a middle-class step too far. Underestimating the demands of small babies is a common error of first-time parents as Kate and William soon realised. Instead of the peaceful bonding time they anticipated at home in Nottingham Cottage, their two-bedroom apartment in Kensington Palace, baby George started life as a restless, crying, very hungry baby and both parents had an almost sleepless night. They received the Queen the following morning, then left London for Kate's family home and the welcome and experienced arms of her mother. For several weeks Carole Middleton helped with the feeding, settling George when he cried and making sure Kate got some rest. She relaxed more easily there than in Kensington Palace with its formality,and watchful eyes of courtiers. As with many new parents those early weeks were a time of trial and error, getting some things right and others wrong.

# *Ten*

# Parenting their way

WILLIAM AND KATE HAD CLEARLY UNDERESTIMATED THE demands of a new-born and the early weeks were testing. William told CAA TV in August that George was 'a bit of a rascal' and 'a little fighter – he wriggles around quite a lot and he doesn't want to go to sleep that much.' He admitted that Kate, who wanted to breast-feed for at least six months, did most of the night feeds but that he had changed the baby's nappy. One of their small misjudgments high-lighted the difference between what can be appropriate for a middle-class family but not for royalty. Many grandfathers take photographs of their baby grandchildren for the family album, but Michael Middleton's pictures of George and his parents that were released to the world's media were deemed not of sufficient high quality for a future king and heavily criticised. It was a lesson William and Kate took on board: they asked Jason Bell, a professional photographer, to take subsequent photo shoots for worldwide consumption during George's first year.

Adapting to parenthood was a challenge for William and Kate just as it is for most couples as they come to terms with the difference between theories of child rearing and reality. They reassessed their ability to handle George, the pressure it was putting on Kate's mother and what was expected of them as senior royals. 'After much thought and deliberation' they agreed they needed some help. William asked one of his childhood nannies, Jessie Webb, then a mature 71, to be George's nanny until the end of the year. She agreed to come out of retirement and accompanied William, Kate and George to Anglesey, where they had lived since 2010. A few weeks later they took their first flight together using a Cessna 750 lent to them by the Duke of Westminster to fly to Balmoral, the Queen's Scottish residence, so that George could meet his great-grandfather, the Duke of Edinburgh.

In September William announced that he was leaving his job as a search-and-rescue pilot with the Royal Air Force to have a 'transitional period' of about a year. Few middle-class new fathers can afford to do this but William, who was carefully selecting a pick and mix lifestyle from both the royal and middle-class worlds, took advantage of his status to opt out of most royal duties and his job to learn what he felt was much more crucial to his personal development: how to be a father.

Establishing a close bond with George, one he didn't experience as a child with his own father, is part of this process and also no doubt also reminds him of his emotional closeness with his mother. Although William was criticised by some for not helping his elderly grandparents with royal duties more than he would be doing, he was concentrating on developing a different aspect of himself that would undoubtedly help heal his damaged childhood and make him a very different type of king.

It wasn't until mid-July 2015 that he returned to being a pilot, this time for the charity East Anglian Air Ambulance. He donated his salary to the charity. He admitted at the start of his first nine-and-a-half-hour shift to 'feeling the nerves' and added: 'It's sort of a follow-on from where I was in the military with my search and rescue role. There are many of the same kind of skills and a job like this is very worthwhile, valuable and there's an element of duty.' His comment perhaps indicates that his fascination with a middle-class lifestyle is not because he wants to avoid his destiny as king but to be a more rounded person.

It's never easy to leave your baby for the first time, and at the Tusk Conservation Awards in September William rather proudly admitted his and Kate's thoughts constantly returned to their son. 'This is actually our first evening out without him,' he confessed. 'So please excuse us if you see us nervously casting surreptitious glances at our mobile phones to check all is well back home.'

William and Kate couldn't stay in their retreat in Anglesey for long; at the start of October they moved into Apartment 1A at Kensington Palace. Princess Margaret used to live there, but Kate who had overseen the refurbishment of the 21-room residence, rejected her taste for brightly coloured walls for a more modern neutral theme. It cost £4 million, paid for by the Queen from money given to her by the government. William and Kate paid for the internal furnishing like carpets and curtains themselves.

Despite the cost, the couple thought of Kensington Palace as their second home. William wanted George to have 'as normal an upbringing as possible', which was difficult in London. Kate had allegedly been upset by photographs taken of her in jeans and wearing a baseball cap, while she was taking George out for a walk in his pram with Lupo their dog. Amner House is much more secluded and gives them the privacy they crave.

Prince George's christening was arranged for October 23, when he would be three months old. William had been baptised on August 4, 1982 at the age of six weeks, while the Prince of Wales was one month and one day old at his own christening. The Queen was five weeks old when she was christened. William once again defied tradition by choosing the Chapel Royal, in St James's Palace, for the service, making George the first future monarch in modern times not to be baptised at Buckingham Palace. Both William and the Prince of Wales were christened in the Music Room at the Palace, while the Queen, then Princess Elizabeth, was, in 1926, christened in the Palace's private chapel. William made the 'personal decision' to chose the smaller, more intimate Chapel Royal because it was where the coffin of his mother Diana lay before her funeral to allow her family to pay their last respects.

He also chose his mother's good friend Julia Samuel, founder of the Child Bereavement UK charity, to be one of George's seven godparents. The others were Zara Tindall, Princess Anne's daughter, Oliver Baker, a friend of the couple from St Andrews, Emilia Jardine-Paterson, Kate's school friend from Marlborough, Jamie Lowther-Pinkerton, William's private secretary, Earl Grosvenor, and William van Cutsem, two of William's long-term friends.

As if to underline their equal role as parents, William carried George into the chapel, while Kate carried him out once the baptism was over. Dressed in a cream-ruffled coat by Alexander McQueen, Kate looked stylish but tired. The Archbishop of Canterbury officiated at the baptism. Only twenty two guests were invited and there was no carriage procession. George wore a replica of the royal baptism lace-and-satin gown first worn by Queen Victoria's eldest daughter, and to his parents' relief behaved impeccably. No doubt William who had said his son had 'a voice to match any lion's roar', was relieved. The Prince of Wales and the Duchess of Cornwall hosted a post-ceremony tea. The official photographs of four generations of the monarchy, together with the Middletons, was a rare arrangement of royals and commoners. It was William's wish, but made some senior royals feel less than comfortable.

The decision where to spend Christmas was looming. It has always been important to the Queen that her family gathers around her at Sandringham, but it is not a relaxing affair. Those who attend are required to adhere to court protocol, including bowing or curtseying to their royal superiors and paying attention to who enters a room first. The Queen usually arrives a day before her guests, but other arrivals are based on seniority, with junior members arriving first and Prince Charles and Camilla arriving last. The family traditionally open their presents, displayed in the Red Drawing Room, in order of royal seniority, on Christmas Eve. Jokey rather than expensive presents are encouraged.

Guests are not expected to entertain themselves. There is a strictly-timed schedule, and invitees are given a list of activities when they arrive. They cannot go to bed before the Queen, who usually stays up until midnight. Guests are expected to change their clothes at least three times during the day depending on the activity and to dress formally with jewels at dinner. The Christmas meal is traditional: turkey and all the trimmings.

In December 2012 Kate was still recovering from extreme morning sickness and she and William spent an informal Christmas Day with her family where she could feel less under pressure. Christmas Day 2013 was spent with the royals but Kate and William joined her family to bring in the New Year. Christmas 2014 was one of compromise. William and Kate attended the traditional Christmas Day church service with the Queen and the royal family. They then returned to Amner House to host the Middletons, a decision that raised eyebrows amongst some royal watchers. But William's priority remains Kate and her family and having once established the precedent he knows he will get his own way.

Having been a child in a marriage that went totally wrong, William has become more aware of what makes a marriage go right. He has established the foundation for a less stressful life and done an enormous amount of soul-searching. He is grateful for the chance to offer his own children a more emotionally stable and demonstrative upbringing than the distant one of his parents and his own stormy childhood. He has also kept his promise to himself that being a hands-on father was a top priority. He may well be a monarch who, unlike his grandmother who priorities her royal duties, puts the needs of the nation on as equal a footing as possible to those of his family.

Kate and William had agreed to go on an official tour of Australia and New Zealand in April 2014. They were determined not to leave George behind but accepted they needed a full-time nanny to look after him. Enter Spanish-born Maria Teresa Turrion Borallo, then 43. She came recommended by a friend and her credentials include being expertly trained at Norland College in Bath. Among other things she also had experience in self-defense, high-speed driving and dealing with paparazzi. She began the job in March and had a month to settle in before they left for the tour. The plan was that Prince George would attend one event in New Zealand and one in Australia. William also insisted they flew as a family. It was another breach of protocol as direct heirs to the throne rarely travel together. The Queen's permission had to be asked, but as she had originally agreed to Diana's wish that she, Charles and William travel together to Australia, there was little option for her but to grant this request.

Taking a child who is not yet one to the other side of the world was always going to have its tricky moments. One of these was watching Kate juggle the wriggling, sturdy George down the steps of the plane that flew them to New Zealand in a strong wind while also trying to keep her hat on and her skirt down.

William admitted to being nervous about how George would cope with the long-haul flight, the tropical climate, and the intense media interest. He told the wife of a serviceman during a state reception in Sydney that George was like a miniature tornado wreaking havoc back at Admiralty House where the family was staying with the governor-general. 'I've been a bit concerned he was destroying everything,' he said. At another reception he remarked that his son was 'at his most vocal at three a.m,' adding, 'I hope that George doesn't keep you up. He's a bonny lad and you'll be pleased to know that he's currently preparing for life as a [rugby] prop forward.'

George's welfare was considered throughout. Very few evening engagements were scheduled on the official tour so that William and Kate could be home for George's bath and bedtime. The couple spent just two nights away from him. Although George's appearances were strictly limited, once on show he instantly became a crowd-stopper and outshone everyone, even his glamorous mother, with his cheeky smile, obvious energy and irresistible range of expressions that extended from sulkiness to mischief. On a play date with other babies of the same age at Government House in Wellington he tried to grab every toy he could including one from a little girl that he flung firmly on to the floor, causing the child to cry. Nanny Borallo was present but stood against a wall in the room, perhaps unsure quite how much she was expected to get involved. At the end of the visit George made up for any mischief by leaning his head lovingly into his mother's neck for a cuddle. He was equally entertaining on his other appearance, an Easter Sunday trip to Taronga Zoo in Sydney. He was fascinated by a bilby – a furry marsupial native to Australia – named George, but had no interest in the official gift from the Governor General of Australia of a cuddly toy wombat which he immediately threw on the ground. Kate and William were so relaxed that they roared with laughter.

Much to William's delight both George and the trip were a huge hit and rekindled an affection the royal family had feared it might not see again in Australia following the death of Princess Diana. The warmth shown to them both as individuals and as a family touched them profoundly and they took the opportunity of George's birthday to show their overall gratitude. Their message read: 'We would like to take this opportunity on George's first birthday to thank everyone over the last year, wherever we have met them, both at home and overseas, for their warm and generous good wishes to George and our family.'

It was an important milestone. A birthday party was arranged and his great-grandmother, the Queen, agreed to come. Prince Charles, who had missed Prince William's first birthday, as he and Princess Diana were on tour in Canada, was this time in Scotland on official duties. Nor could Prince Phillip make it, so before the celebration Kate, accompanied by her nanny and a police protection officer, drove George to Buckingham Palace so he could see his great-grandson on his special day. Kate's parents, however, were the first guests to arrive. They must at times feel they are dreaming that a future king of England wants them to have such an important role in the life of his heir.

George has since made the occasional, carefully selected appearance. He was tremendously excited by the Trooping the Colour ceremony on June 13, 2015 – to mark the Queens's 89th birthday – which he watched from a window of Buckingham Palace in the safe arms of Nanny Borrallo. The occasion also marked Kate's first public outing since the birth of Princess Charlotte. George also watched the traditional RAF flypast from the balcony of Buckingham Palace, this time in Prince William's arms. He enthusiastically pointed at the planes and even waved at the crowds below. He also showed a tender side to his nature in the photographs that Kate took of him and four-week-old baby Charlotte, when he held her tiny hand and kissed her gently on the forehead. It was yet another break with royal protocol but unlike her father's portraits these were a triumph of domestic photography and received universal acclaim.

# Eleven
## A united family

KATE'S SECOND PREGNANCY WAS ANNOUNCED ON SEPTEMBER 8, 2014. It became public knowledge early as Kate once again was suffering from hyperemesis gravidarium, the severe form of pregnancy sickness that made the first trimester of her pregnancy with George so difficult. This time she was not admitted to hospital but treated by doctors at Kensington Palace. At a public engagement in Oxford on the day her pregnancy was announced Prince William told reporters: 'Kate is feeling OK. It's been a tricky few days, week or so. But we're immensely thrilled. It's great news. Early days. Hopefully things settle down and she feels a bit better.'

Prince Charles reacted to the news by telling well-wishers that he hoped this time the baby would be a girl. Kate subsequently pulled out of all royal duties, including a trip to Malta which would have marked her first solo trip abroad. By late October she was feeling better, and appeared in public again. Two months later she and William made a three-day official visit to New York leaving Prince George with her parents.

The Lindo Wing of St Mary's Hospital was again chosen for the royal baby's birth. Alan Farthing, a consultant gynaecological surgeon, and Guy Thorpe-Beeston, a consultant obstetrician, were in charge of the delivery. Both men had been on duty when Prince George was born. Also on hand was Sunit Godambe, a consultant neonatologist who had checked the health of baby George as soon as he was born.

Kate went into hospital around 6am on May 2, 2015, and her daughter was born at 8.34am. As it was her second baby she probably stayed at Kensington Palace during the early stages of labour while keeping in close touch with her medical team at the hospital. William was again with her. The baby weighed 8 pounds 3 ounces, three ounces less than her brother. As the second child of the Duke and Duchess of Cambridge she is fourth in line to the throne. Kensington Palace press office issued a press release on the morning of her birth to inform the world's media that 'The Duchess of Cambridge had been safely delivered of a daughter.'

A few hours later Prince George was brought to the hospital by his father to see his mother and meet his baby sister. His blond hair had obviously been well brushed and he was dressed smartly in blue and white that colour-coordinated with his father. When he got out of the car the little boy took one look at the crowd and rows of photographers, frowned in disbelief and tugged urgently at his father's leg. William immediately got the message, lifted him up in his arms and whispered words of encouragement. George then waved to the crowd from the safety of his father's arms. William kissed him tenderly. It was a heart-melting moment that showed that William is no longer inhibited about expressing his emotions in public.

Less than twelve hours after the birth, Kate with a beaming William at her side was photographed on the steps of the Lindo Wing for the short drive back to Kensington Palace. She looked stunning in a yellow and white patterned Jenny Packham dress, was perfectly made up and her hair had been styled. Mothers shared their disbelief on Twitter asking how she did it. It was a clear example of how determined she can be, a characteristic that helped her wait for William to propose and has since enabled her to make him her absolute priority and not let him down in her royal duties.

Managing grandparents' expectations and making sure each side gets their own special time with a grandchild is part of parenthood and not always easy. It was obviously going to be more complicated for William and Kate not only because of the significant social divide between the middle-class Middletons and Prince Charles, particularly as the prince is a stickler for protocol and used to 'the other side' being virtually ignored once their child marries into the royal family, but also because Kate is so close to her family while Prince Charles is often away on royal business. The balance was so heavily in the Middletons' favour that Prince Charles bemoaned in public that he 'almost never saw' George – a comment that can be interpreted that he may, in some small way, be following William's example and wants to be a better grandfather than he was a father. Prince Charles has also refurbished the tree house in the garden at Highgrove that William and Harry loved to play in when they were young boys, installed a £20,000 hand-made artisan's shepherd's hut that has a little bed and a woodburner, plus provided a plastic tea set for him to play with.

Kate knows William so well that she may have judged the time was right to encourage a greater rapprochement between William and his father and saw George as the ideal catalyst. There is no doubt too now that he is more contented William feels less resentment over his past. He is also very proud of George. The result was that, shortly after Prince Charles's comment, George was taken to Highgrove House, the Prince of Wales's and Duchess of Cornwall's home, near Tetbury, Gloucestershire, to spend time with his grandfather. Prince Charles was delighted and helped George plant a lime sapling in the kitchen garden with his small trowel and mini-sized watering can.

It is also possible to discern a subtle and distinct change of view. Although William and Kate want George to have as near normal an upbringing as possible the reality is that there is obviously more to bringing up a child who is heir to the throne than merely absorbing middle-class values from his maternal grand-parents. Prince George needs to learn certain royal traditions and practices from an early age to prepare him gently for his destiny. He also has to accept the fact that wherever he goes he will be accompanied by protection officers. It is something the Middletons understandably know precious little about. Perhaps George, as young as he is, is instinctively already beginning to understand the difference between what is expected of him at a formal royal occasion and the freedom he has with his close family. He was, for example, apart from a brief show of tears, very well-behaved at Princess Charlotte's christening.

The occasion's mixture of intimacy and grandeur showed that Kate and William are working hard to keep the balance right. On the one hand, they accepted their senior royal status. This time Nanny Borello was not kept in the background but was prominent in her brown Norland Nanny uniform, and had the important job of looking after William during the christening. On the other hand, William insisted that the Middletons fea-tured prominently in the official photographs of the christening.

It seems clear that he and Kate will adhere to some royal tra-ditions, ignore others and create a few of their own. He under-lined his respect for royal traditional and the Queen while also acknowledging his own destiny in a preface to Lord Douglas Hurd's biography called Elizabeth II: The Steadfast published in August 2015. He wrote: 'All of us who will inherit the legacy of my grandmother's reign and generation need to do all we can to celebrate and learn from her story. 'Speaking for myself, I am privileged to have the Queen as a model for a life of service to the public.'

If Prince George felt at all put out by Princess Charlotte being the focus of so much attention at the christening, it was his turn in the spotlight a couple of weeks later when he celebrated his second birthday. Guests at his party included his great-grand-parents, the Queen and Prince Philip. Prince William could attend too as he had a rest day from work. Missing were Prince Charles and Camilla, who were on a royal tour of the West Country, and Prince Harry, who was doing charity work in Namibia. To underline the little prince's royal status, the bells at Westminster Abbey pealed at lunchtime, and the Grenadier Guards at Buckingham Palace played 'Happy Birthday' during the Changing of the Guard.

The effect on William of being a father has been enormous. 'It is fantastic having a lovely little family and I am so thrilled,' he said on the day he started his new job as an air ambulance pilot. 'Catherine has been doing an amazing job as a mother and I'm very proud of her.' Perhaps too it was his way of silencing those critics who say Kate is not pulling her weight and choosing her royal duties to suit herself. Certainly some royal watchers felt she was wrong to turn up at the Wimbledon tennis championships in July 2015 but not join William in Hyde Park the previous day for the poignant memorial service with families and survivors of the 7/7 London bombing attacks in 2005. But William has shown his belief that at this stage of their lives Kate has a far more important job bringing up their children in a loving and supportive home, one that will also ensure a stable future king, than turning up at countless royal events.

One aide even made the snide comment that William and Kate were spending so much time at their country retreat on the Sandringham estate that they had become 'almost semi-detached royals.' William is unlikely to bend to this criticism. He wants his children brought up as far removed as possible from the pressures and influence of palace life, surrounded by servants and followed by the paparazzi that he remembers only too well from his own childhood, especially once his parents had divorced. Although there are inevitable security checks at Amner House, he can completely relax there and when he is home he is likely to turn up in the kitchen to make his own cup of coffee rather than call a servant.

Such ordinary events in the life of this extraordinary young man will affect his kingdom, as well as himself. Prince George and his sister will create the next link in a different type of chain that will strengthen not only his own position as future king but that of future generations of British royals. As George grows up he will naturally be at ease in a more informal environment and benefit from being part of a close family. William's contentment in his family is well-deserved. In retrospect it is extraordinary that when only eighteen he had the self-knowledge and insight to recognise what he needed both to heal himself and in turn to preserve the monarchy. That he remained determined to go through with it, however tough it was at first, is a remarkable accomplishment.

# *Epilogue*
## A different royal future

No one can know what the future holds, but William's story is one of hope triumphing over experience and the redemption of a broken family. It is notoriously difficult to break the cycle of inherited dysfunction, and credit is due to Charles and Diana that William seems to have made this crucial break, but above all to William himself.

His story also shows that there is nothing inevitable about the malignant cycle of family breakdown. The antidote to it can be the traditional family: mother, father, and children, with their feet firmly on the ground. It is what William gravitated towards in Kate and the Middletons. This unremarkable middle-class family could be the saving of William – and his babies could mark the final closure of a history of misery and the beginning of a new and healthy family. We will also see the fruition of a seed that Diana, Princess of Wales, for all her faults, sowed in William, which he will now pass on, in a richer and deeper way, to his own children. His babies will perhaps be just as much hers as his.

# Acknowledgements

My thanks are due to Melanie Philips whose idea this book was and who gave me the original commission; to Martin Colyer for designing it; and to my husband Robert Low for his patience and professional help. I also wish to thank the many sources who provided background information but who, understandably, prefer to remain anonymous.

Made in the USA
Monee, IL
30 May 2023